Modern Development of the Dry Fly

MODERN DEVELOPMENT OF
THE DRY FLY

The late Edgar Williamson.

Modern Development
of the
Dry Fly

THE NEW DRY FLY PATTERNS

THE MANIPULATION OF DRESSING THEM

AND

PRACTICAL EXPERIENCES OF THEIR USE

BY

FREDERIC M. HALFORD

'DETACHED BADGER' OF *THE FIELD*

AUTHOR OF

'FLOATING FLIES AND HOW TO DRESS THEM'
'DRY FLY FISHING IN THEORY AND PRACTICE'
'DRY FLY ENTOMOLOGY'
'MAKING A FISHERY'
AND
'AN ANGLER'S AUTOBIOGRAPHY'

NEW YORK

E. P. DUTTON AND COMPANY

LONDON: GEORGE ROUTLEDGE AND SONS, LIMITED

Modern Development
of the
Dry Fly

THE NEW DRY FLY PATTERNS

THE MANIPULATION OF DRESSING THEM

AND

PRACTICAL EXPERIENCES OF THEIR USE

BY

FREDERIC M. HALFORD

'DETACHED BADGER' OF *THE FIELD*

AUTHOR OF

'FLOATING FLIES AND HOW TO DRESS THEM'
'DRY FLY FISHING IN THEORY AND PRACTICE'
'DRY FLY ENTOMOLOGY'
'MAKING A FISHERY'
AND
'AN ANGLER'S AUTOBIOGRAPHY'

NEW YORK
E. P. DUTTON AND COMPANY
LONDON: GEORGE ROUTLEDGE AND SONS, LIMITED

First Printed in 1910

Printed by BALLANTYNE, HANSON & CO.
At the Ballantyne Press, Edinburgh

CONTENTS

PART I

THE HALFORD DRY FLY PATTERNS

PART II

THE HALFORD DRY FLY PATTERNS IN USE

LIST OF PLATES

PART I

PART II

MODERN DEVELOPMENT OF THE DRY FLY

PART I

CHAPTER I

THE ORIGIN OF THE NEW PATTERNS

TOWARDS the end of 1901 my friend, the late Edgar Williamson, hearing that I was on the look-out for some fishing, made me a most liberal offer which enabled me to join him on the length of the Itchen, which he rented at St. Cross; and for the remainder of his life I had the gratification of following my favourite sport in the congenial company of one of the most charming of men and one of the very best of sportsmen. He had for many years been a firm believer in the paramount importance of reproducing in each part of the artificial fly the precise shade of colour of the same part of the natural insect, and at the same time dressing a fly as nearly as possible of the exact size and shape of the living subimago or imago.

A

His persistent and logical advocacy of this theory impressed me very much, and impelled me to try and design a number of flies for use on the south country and other chalk streams which would carry out in detail his well-conceived ideas. He was one who never spared himself whether in business or in sport, and being naturally a delicate man, his health unfortunately gave way under the strain, and on the 21st of March 1904 he passed away, to the intense grief of a large circle of sympathising friends. It should be recognised by one and all that any improvement in the sport of the dry-fly man effected by the use of these new patterns is primarily due to him as the originator of the idea, and I therefore think that the portrait of the late Edgar Williamson is the most appropriate frontispiece for this volume.

I am desirous of placing on record here my own views on the colour question, views which I am told are shared by many others. I am not, and never have been, a believer in the theory advanced some years since by Sir Herbert Maxwell that fish are colour-blind. In justice to him it should be said that he himself has since, to a great degree, recanted some of the opinions he advanced on the subject. While believing that the trout or grayling in the water can, to some extent, differentiate tones and colours, I do not think that the presence or absence, say, for example, of a tinge of brown in the body of a female iron-blue spinner would suffice to account for a trout feeding on the natural insect (*Baëtis pumilus*) represented by this pattern, fastening to the one with this brown shade, and coming short to one dressed with claret body like the old-fashioned pattern. At the same time, there are occasions when, and places where, one is almost tempted to think that the colour perception of the Salmonidæ is developed to the highest degree. Every fisherman, however, who has devoted himself to the entomological side of the question, and has also been interested in working out and dressing patterns of flies, must feel a great satisfaction in turning out one which is a truer and better imitation of nature than the generality of those he had seen before. No doubt he will fish this improved pattern with a fuller sense of confidence in its efficacy than he would with an inferior imitation, and, as has been so often written before, confidence in a particular fly is one of the most potent factors tending to render it successful in use.

During the fishing season of 1902 every available moment at the river-side was devoted by me to collecting a very large number of specimens of the flies on which the rising trout feed freely. These specimens were sorted into genera and species, the Ephemeridæ into subimagines and imagines, and the sexes separated. As soon as a sufficient number of a sex of a particular insect had been collected they were carefully and exhaustively examined, with a view of arriving at typical specimens of the bulk. Setting aside solitary abnormal examples, the variations of size and colour are not generally very great, and it was therefore evident at an early stage in the investigations that an enormous proportion were to all intents and purposes identical, and from these the specimens to be imitated were selected.

I wish to lay great stress on this point, because friends often tell me that on a particular day a particular fly on a particular stream was larger or smaller, paler or darker, than my patterns. On cross-examination it appears that these opinions are generally based on casual observation of one or two specimens. It has been laid down by an eminent entomologist that no one ought to describe an insect for scientific purposes until he has examined under the microscope at least 200 examples, and in all text-books, when describing a rare insect, the fact is prominently set forth that only a few examples have been secured. Any one wishing to get out new patterns should be actuated by a similar sense of the responsibility of jumping at conclusions from insufficient data, and should ever keep steadfastly in view the principle that standard patterns must be dressed to imitate as faithfully as possible the most plentiful and therefore normal size, shape, and colouring.

Most of the previous attempts to match the form and colour of the Ephemeridæ have failed, because dry specimens shrivel up rapidly, losing both shape and colour, and until lately no method of preserving satisfactorily either form or colour in fluid had been discovered.

In an article published in the *Field* of April
27, 1901, a number of experiments with formalin
were described, and for convenience the procedure
is briefly recapitulated here, as, so far, it has not been
found possible to effect any great improvement in it.
Two solutions are made—firstly, the collecting fluid;
and secondly, the preserving fluid. The former
consists of one-third rectified spirits of wine or
alcohol, and two-thirds of a 2 per cent. aqueous
solution of formalin, to which as many crystals of
menthol as will dissolve are added. The preserving fluid is simply a 2 per cent. aqueous solution
of formalin. The solutions must both be carefully
filtered before use. Formalin is a trade name given
to a preparation which is a 40 per cent. aqueous
solution of formic aldehyde, and what is usually called
a 2 per cent. solution of formalin is made by adding
1 fluid ounce of the formalin to 19 fluid ounces of
water, to make in all 20 fluid ounces, or an imperial
pint. Although it is usual to describe this as 2 per
cent. formalin, it will be seen that it is a misnomer,
as, in fact, it is a 5 per cent. solution of formalin,
or a 2 per cent. solution of formic aldehyde.

The Ephemeridæ or other insects as taken from
the water are dropped into the collecting fluid, and,
as soon as convenient after they are completely immersed, are transferred to the preserving fluid. In
any case this transference should take place within six
hours after the capture of the fly, especially in cases
where the preservation of colour is of importance.

I must strenuously impress upon the student the absolute necessity of taking every individual specimen from the surface of the stream. To collect at haphazard Ephemeridæ in the air, or from the grass or boughs of the trees and shrubs, and then imitate them, would, to say the least, be unwise, and for two reasons—firstly, because the duns and spinners are continually changing their colours during the brief span of their life in the winged stages on the earth; and secondly, because it is only at certain and well-defined stages that they are voluntarily on or under the surface of the stream, and the trout and grayling (with, of course, fish like dace, chub, roach, and perch) only see them in any great numbers, and are, therefore, tempted to feed on them, at these particular stages.

Thus the dun or subimago as it emerges from the nymphal envelope is on the water, it flies ashore as soon as it can—that is, when its wings are dry—and from this stage to that of oviposition by the female in the spinner or imago state, remains ashore unless blown on to the water by a sudden, irresistible gust of wind—a circumstance which is, to say the least, unusual. The next stage at which the fish are likely to see and feed on the Ephemeridæ is during oviposition, when the female imago is just touching the surface of the stream to wash a number of eggs off the hinder segments of the abdomen, or when a similar female is descending into the water to deposit the eggs in a suitable position and then returning to the surface. Lastly, both male and female imago, having completed the essential work of their lifetime, that of procreation, fall almost lifeless on the water, and the wings droop until they assume a horizontal position, lie flat on the surface, and the spinners, floating down the stream, are once more in a position to attract the attention of the feeding fish in the river.

Another, and in some respects a paramount, advantage to be derived from collecting and imitating the insects only at these stages is that the number of patterns required to complete the outfit of the modern dry-fly fisherman has thus been reduced within something like reasonable limits. In my previous books I must plead guilty to having offended in this respect. In "Floating Flies and How to Dress Them," published in 1886, there are 9 patterns of mayflies and spent gnats, and 81 other patterns, or 90 in all; and in "Dry Fly Entomology," published in 1897, the title of Part II. is "The Hundred Best Patterns of Floating Flies." The number of patterns contained in the new set consists of 4 mayflies, 2 spent gnats, and 27 other patterns, or 33 in all; and except for the addition of the grannom in the case of the few rivers in which this spring example of the Trichoptera is still plentiful, these are, to my mind, quite sufficient patterns for any dry-fly man on a south country or other chalk stream.

Some of my readers may express surprise at

the omission from the list of all the so-called *fancy* patterns.   Of course, if an experienced fisherman has implicit belief in the efficacy of a wickham, a bumble, a red tag, or any other fancy fly, he must add it to his list, because, as before said, I am quite convinced that nothing tends to success with a particular fly more surely than this implicit belief in its efficacy.

The following paragraph is from an article in the *Field* of April 25, 1903· "It may be remembered that in the latter part of last year an article from my pen treated of the new patterns which had been worked out here by me with the local fly-dresser—patterns in which a serious attempt had been made to try and reproduce as nearly as possible the precise shades of colour in the natural insect.   At the time I warned my readers that it was premature to infer that, because they are presumably a better match in colour than any previous imitations, they would prove more killing.   The limited experience of last season, however, has been so encouraging that I have decided, metaphorically, to burn my boats for this season, so as to try the experiment fully."

During 1903, 1904, 1905, 1906, 1907, 1908, and 1909 I fished the Itchen and Test with the new patterns only—in fact, since the first of these seven years I have no other flies in the boxes carried at the river-side.   Looking back and considering the question in the most judicial frame of mind, I cannot find that I have on any occasion been placed at a disadvantage by limiting myself to their use. On many days, and under varying climatic and other conditions, I am clearly of opinion that the natural appearance of the artificial flies has largely contributed to any modicum of success I may have achieved with the shy trout and grayling of the pellucid chalk streams. A later part of this book will be devoted to considering in detail some of the cases in which I deem the excellence of the patterns to have appreciably conduced to an amelioration of the sport.

CHAPTER II

MATCHING THE COLOURS, SIZES, AND RELATIVE PROPORTIONS

THE typical specimens to be imitated having been selected from the bulk, each one is placed back downwards in a small white porcelain saucer, evaporating dish, colour pan, or other suitable receptacle, containing a small quantity of the 2 per cent. formalin or preserving fluid. A white vessel is to be preferred for this purpose, because, as the result of a large number of experiments, it would seem that the tints can be better seen and matched against a white background than against one of any other colour. The insects are placed on their backs so as to expose the ventral surface to view, because, whether in the subimago state of the Ephemeridæ with wings erect, or in the imago state of members of the same family after the work of procreation has been accomplished, when the wings are usually outspread and flat at right angles to the line of the body, they are almost invariably displayed to the fish from this point of view.

In the same way the flies belonging to the other families of water-bred insects which serve as food for the fish are usually seen in a similar position,

i.e. with the ventral portion of the body in juxtaposition to the surface of the water; but in the case
of these the wings—four in the Trichoptera and two
in the Diptera, &c.—are set on at an angle of
approximately 30° to the horizontal, more or less in
penthouse form, with the apices lying close together
and the root ends at the sides of the thorax.

The matching of the colours has now to be
accomplished. To examine and match colours of
parts of small objects like the natural insects with
the naked eye is practically impossible, and an achromatic lens of small magnification, with a flat field,
must be used for this purpose. Nothing has as
yet been made so admirably adapted to the work
as the Zeiss Aplanatic, × 6. Being made of the
very finest and most modern optical (Abbé-Schott)
glass, it is perfectly achromatic, and the combination
having been calculated and worked out by the
highest German scientific authorities on the subject,
there is a marked superiority in quality and in
flatness of field over any other lens yet known
or sold.

A few words of comment on the effect of dis-
playing the insects against the white background
will not be out of place. It is doubtful whether a
fish looking up at a fly floating on the surface against
the clear sky can, to any extent, differentiate delicate
gradations of colour. Viewed against an opaque
background, such as a bridge crossing the river or
an overhanging bank, the colour is no doubt better

defined to the fish. If the trout or grayling can distinguish the colour of any part of the fly which is opaque, it must be the colour of the ventral portion. On the other hand, if the part of the fly visible to the fish is to any degree transparent, the colour of the darker or dorsal side of it must to some extent affect the transparent shade, and the more transparent this visible part of the fly, the greater must be the effect of the darker dorsal portion in the fish's eyes. I would urge that the colour of any part of the fly, whether opaque or transparent, as seen against the background of the white saucer, will, as nearly as possible, reproduce these conditions; and hence the colours of the various parts of the artificial flies, in so far as they can be distinguished by the fish, will appear to them of the same shade as that of the insect when thus displayed

In the case of the first set of patterns designed by me, the material to dress each part of each fly was carefully selected from the stock of Mr. G. Holland, the fly-dresser, who was at that time located in Winchester; and where I could not find suitable material or material of the requisite colour, we discussed thoroughly the nature of the material to be used, and he proceeded at once to dye samples one after the other until the exact shade was obtained. The pattern flies were then tentatively tied by his son, and of those that did not at first come out satisfactorily further patterns were dressed, until at last I passed them as correct in colour, size, and shape. The assistance thus rendered at this stage of the experiment was of great use, and I feel it due to them that this fact should be recorded here.

During 1903 and 1904 many of the patterns were more or less modified. Continual comparison of the artificial with the natural fly gave opportunities for correcting the colours, substituting more suitable for less suitable materials, and generally improving them and making them more effective and better imitations of the natural insect. In 1905 I migrated to the Test, and there made a further number of comparisons between the patterns and the insects they were intended to represent, and I may here note that it was a matter of deep gratification to find that prolonged observation only tended to confirm the opinion I had long held that in colour, size, and form the flies of the Test were identical with the same species on the Itchen

The class of materials to be selected for the manufacture of the various parts of the artificial fly is a question deserving of careful study and consideration. Silk, which in olden times was used for the bodies of many standard patterns, is quite out of date. Immersion in water effects a startling change in the shades of colour of silk bodies, invariably darkening them, and in many cases quite changing the colour. Thus, for example, white floss silk when wetted becomes a slaty grey, many of the yellows assume an olive tint, and all the olive silks darken so much that the very palest shades of olive silk procurable are, when soaked, dark enough for the darkest of olives in the natural insect.

All that has been written on the alteration of the colours effected by immersion in water of silk can be repeated as to the effect of paraffin, with the addition that the darkening of the shade and alteration of colour is even more prominent and pronounced when the paraffin used nowadays to waterproof the dry-fly fisherman's patterns is applied. Yet the advantage of the use of paraffin is so obvious that few dry-fly men in the present age would think their outfit complete without the paraffin bottle and brush.

Dubbing is the name given by fly-dressers to fibres of fur, wool, or other animal hair, either dyed or in their natural colours and picked to pieces. When necessary, two or more sorts are picked out together to blend them thoroughly and get the correct colouring. For the body, and in some patterns the legs, of the sunk fly dubbing is an ideal material, because of its transparent, watery, and life-like appearance ; also because, when wetted, there is little if any change of colour. It is not, however, a suitable substance for the bodies of floating flies, as patterns dressed with it, when once thoroughly soaked, are difficult to dry ; a fly with its body sodden cannot float well, and the use of dubbing has for these reasons been quite superseded by the modern school of dry-fly dressers.

Quill, horsehair, and Rofia grass, either dyed or undyed, are the materials to be preferred for dressing the bodies of floating flies. To match the colours with those of the natural insect, the body or other material to be used should be immersed in the preserving fluid, placed close to the part of the insect which it is intended to represent, and the colour carefully matched under the lens. Size is, of course, an essential feature of the work, and the hook to be selected should have the length of its shank as nearly as possible equal to the length of the abdomen and thorax of the natural insect. The wings of the Ephemeridæ are approximately the same length as the hook-shank of the artificial, or the abdomen and thorax of the living fly.

If the body and thorax are of two or more colours or shades, their relative proportions can be noted and reproduced. In the male spinners of the olive, pale watery. and iron-blue the bodies are in three sections of different colours, the hindermost two or three segments of one colour, the rest of the abdomen a white or pale transparent tint, and the thorax dark brown or nearly black. The bodies of these patterns are made of horsehair, either white or dyed to the respective shades, and a convenient method of keeping the sections of uniform width is to count and note the number of turns of each on the hook-shank. The turbinate eyes of the male spinners are bright yellow, cadmium yellow, orange or red brown, and two or three turns of horsehair dyed to the requisite tint are wound round the neck of the hook to represent these.

CHAPTER III

SELECTION AND ARRANGEMENT OF THE SERIES

IT is impossible to exaggerate the importance to
the modern dry-fly fisherman of having at the river-
side a complete series of imitations of the flies which
are freely taken as food by the rising fish. It must
be conceded that to select and arrange in some logical
order of sequence the number required to constitute a
full equipment, and yet not overburden him with an
inordinate quantity of patterns, is a matter of some
difficulty.

The old school of angling writers generally
arranged their flies according to the month in which
the particular species were present in considerable
numbers. Although there are, no doubt, many arguments to be adduced in favour of such a plan, yet
I confess it never appealed to me very forcibly. On
the Test, Itchen, and similar chalk streams, some flies,
like the olive and iron-blue duns and their spinners,
are practically abundant during the entire fishing
season. Others, like the pale watery dun, blue-winged
olive, and their respective imagines, do not commence
hatching out in any number before, say, the middle
of June, and continue to be on the water more or less
up to the end of the season. Some of the black

gnats and curses or smuts are, "like the poor, always with us," and the mayflies are only seen in quantity in parts of certain streams during, say, a fortnight from the third week or end of May.

The mayfly has no doubt achieved a great reputation—greater in many respects than it ever deserved. It has, however, of late years shown distinct signs of decline, and, in the opinion of many observers, is likely in the near future to be a rarity on the south-country chalk streams, if indeed it does not become extinct. Whether this should be a source of regret is a question which is arguable, but I do not think that this volume is the place to reproduce the multifarious opinions on the subject. Here the various patterns imitating it have been given the seat of honour and are placed at the head of the list.

There are three authenticated species of true mayfly to be found in the British Isles—*Ephemera danica*, *Ephemera vulgata*, and *Ephemera lineata*. Examination of many hundreds of specimens from the Test has only revealed the presence of one of these, viz. *E. danica;* but all three have been taken on the Itchen. It will suffice for the fly-dresser to know that the subimago of *E. danica* is of a greener tint in the wings, and generally paler, than the other two species. *E. vulgata* and *E. lineata* in the subimago stage are practically identical in colouration, much browner in the wings, and generally darker and slightly larger, than *E. danica*. In all the Ephemeridæ the males are considerably smaller than the

B

females. Nos. 1 and 2, the green mayfly, male and female, are imitations of the subimago of *E. danica*, and Nos. 3 and 4, the brown mayfly, male and female, are intended to represent the subimagines of *E. vulgata* or *E. lineata*. The colouration of the imagines is so similar in all three species that it has not been deemed necessary to unduly multiply the number of patterns by dressing separate imitations, and Nos. 5 and 6 are accordingly the imagines or spent gnat of all the British species of the genus Ephemera.

Probably the olive dun and its spinners are the most plentiful of the Ephemeridæ on the Hampshire chalk streams and many other British rivers No. 7 of the new series of patterns is the olive dun male, and No. 8 the female, of the same fly, Nos. 9 and 10 being the male and female respectively of the dark olive dun. These two distinct shades of olive, of which the dark is distinctly of a darker and browner shade in the body, legs, and whisk, and the wings darker and bluer than the ordinary olive, are frequently on the water at the same time. Some day, I hope to be able to determine whether they are distinct species, or merely variations of *Baetis vernus* or *B. rhodani*. When they are both present, I think the dark olive is, as a rule, not so well taken by the fish as the common olive.

No. 11 is the olive spinner male, No. 12 the olive spinner female, and No. 13 the olive (red) spinner female. The two patterns of female imagines are given, because in many cases, while the ovipositing female has the body distinctly olive in colour, the same insect, after depositing its eggs and being what many anglers style *spent* or *burnt*, assumes in the body the dark dead-leaf colour of the pattern No. 13.

I would call my readers' attention to the wings of these patterns, because I think it is due to my friend Williamson to remark that he was largely responsible for the adoption of the hackle points laid on horizontally at right angles to the hook-shank for the wings of all spinners. They are certainly most natural-looking and effective, but a fly dressed in this way requires more drying than the duns with wings of starling or coot pinion feather.

The wings of the imagines of the Ephemeridæ consist of a membrane (which is usually glassy and iridescent) and opaque or semi-opaque neuration, varying in colour in different species. I would suggest that the fibres of the hackle represent the longitudinal nervures, while the spaces between the fibres represent the thin transparent membrane of the wings themselves. When hackles are selected for spinner wings, their colour should match as nearly as possible the colour of the wing neuration in the species to be imitated.

Nos. 14 and 15 are the male and female pale watery dun, and Nos. 16 and 17 the spinners of the same fly. There are a considerable number of insects called indiscriminately pale watery duns—*Baetis binoculatus, Baetis scambus, Centroptilum luteolum,* and *Centroptilum pennulatum.* The colouration of these does not vary to any great extent, and the variations are chiefly in the turbinate eyes of the male imago. These are described by Eaton in the species above named, and in the same order in which they are given above—lemon or bright yellow, clove or warm sepia brown, bright light red, and light cadmium orange. I have not thought it necessary to make separate patterns for these variations of colour, but the ultra-purist might perhaps with advantage dress the male spinners of the pale watery with the horsehair wound round the head, varied in colour like the turbinate eyes as described by Rev. A. E. Eaton.

Nos. 18 and 19 are the male and female iron-blue duns, and Nos. 20 and 21 the imagines of the same species. The male spinner of the iron-blue is generally known among anglers as the jenny spinner, but probably is often confused with the male spinners of the olive and pale watery, which are to some degree similar to the imago of the male iron-blue, but differing in the size and in the colours of the thorax and segments of the abdomen.

Nos. 22 and 23 are the two sexes of the blue-winged olive, and Nos. 24 and 25 the imagines (male and female) of this fly, usually called sherry spinners by fishermen.

The foregoing complete the list of Ephemeridæ,

imitations of which are comprised in the series. The march brown is so seldom found in Hampshire chalk streams that I have not had the opportunity of working out patterns to represent it. In parts of the country where it is plentiful it is undoubtedly one of the most important members of the family for the fish and fishermen. It is to be hoped that some enthusiast will devote the necessary time to secure a considerable number of examples of both sexes of it in the subimago and imago stages. One could then undertake the labour of love of matching the colours, size, and proportions, and no doubt succeed in dressing patterns of them which would be good and true imitations of the natural insects.

The yellow may dun (*Heptagenia sulphurea* or *H. flavipennis*) and the turkey brown (*Leptophlebia submarginata*) are sometimes present in considerable numbers, but from the experience of many hundreds of autopsies I cannot find that they are appreciated by the fish.

Smutting fish, *i.e.* fish feeding on the black gnats, fisherman's curse, and other tiny Diptera, more or less black in colour, are to be seen so often in the chalk streams and other rivers that it was absolutely necessary to give some patterns likely to tempt the trout and grayling when taking these annoying little insects. I have found the use of patterns dressed on ooo hooks so disappointing in hooking and holding the fish rising to flies dressed on them, that

tentatively I decided to try and leave out of the
list any patterns requiring these very small hooks.
Probably the fisherman's curse (*Hilara*), the reed
smut (*Simulium*), and the black gnat (*Bibio johannis*)
are the most plentiful flies of this sort to be seen
on the water. The fisherman's curse and reed smut
are so small that no pattern dressed on hooks
larger than ooo are suitable as imitations, and I
have therefore decided to omit them.

The so-called black gnat (which is not a gnat
at all) is at once plentiful and an acceptable morsel
for the feeding trout and grayling, and with a
goodly number of both sexes from which the specimens to be imitated were selected, the working
out of the two patterns, Nos. 26 and 27, the
male and female respectively, presented no great
difficulty, and both of them are dressed on oo
hooks.

Nearly all the fishermen I have met of late years
join me in recording the opinion that fish taking
the smuts or curses, as well as those feeding on
Bibio johannis itself, will rise freely, and under
favourable conditions fasten to the imitations of
the black gnat comprised in the new series. One
of my friends, a very experienced and successful
man with the dry fly, has on various occasions
assured me that he considers the male (No. 26) the
most killing pattern he can find, both on the Test
and Itchen, during the summer weather. He generally calls it *the chab with a red tie*, from the pale

maroon horsehair at the neck, which represents the
turbinate eyes of the male black gnat.

The next pattern on the list, No. 28, is the brown
ant.   The old standard red ant was a very useful
fly, and most successful during the summer and
early autumn.   One afternoon at the end of August
1903 there was an unprecedented flight of winged
ants on the St. Cross water, and the fish were
rising madly at it.   I was at the river-side with a
friend, and felt inclined to try and make a record
among the trout.   With some difficulty I persuaded
myself to resist the temptation, and putting away
the rod, armed myself with a small insect net and
a large bottle of the collecting fluid.   For hours
I literally slaved at securing a great number of
specimens, transferred them as soon as possible
to the preserving fluid, and walked back to Winchester, where we proceeded without delay to work
out a satisfactory imitation.   The result is the
pattern now adopted in the series, and one which
has since earned a great reputation as a killer.

The two patterns Nos. 29 and 30 are the male
and female welshman's button respectively.   They
are imitations of one of the Trichoptera or Caddis-
flies (*Sericostoma personatum*), belonging to the family
of the Sericostomatidæ.   Some of our Welsh friends
are very indignant at the Hampshire nomenclature,
and one writer in the sporting press has made a very
violent attack and abused me in somewhat intem-
perate language for my presumption in differing from

the opinion expressed by him, that the name welsh-man's button has been rightly applied by fishermen to one of the Coleoptera somewhat akin to and resembling the coch-y-bonddhu. For more than thirty years I have fished the south-country chalk streams, and have, whenever able to compare notes with the local keepers and fishermen, found that this Caddis-fly has from time immemorial been called by them the welshman's button. Some of my critics have an idea that the name implies a Welsh origin, and a witty friend has remarked that one might just as well imagine that *plaster of Paris* is only made in the capital of France, or *Roman cement* in the Italian metropolis.

Be it as it may, the welshman's button is to-day a most important fly on the chalk streams, and as its appearance and that of the mayfly are simultaneous, and the latter is fast disappearing, the time has now arrived when during the old mayfly season the most killing pattern is the imitation of *Sericostoma personatum.* In my own experience the male is better taken than the female, but possibly this is in some degree due to the fact that of two patterns of the same fly I always incline towards the smaller, especially in the clear water and with the shy fish of the Test or Itchen.

Another fly classified amongst the Trichoptera, which appears on the water at about the same time as the mayfly and welshman's button is the large red sedge—*Phryganea striata* or *Phryganea grandis*

—the two species being so similar in colour, shape, and size that it is scarcely possible to differentiate the females, and the males are only distinguished by the structural details of the genitalia. I worked out a pattern of the male some years since, but I abandoned it, because it was altogether of such large dimensions that it could scarcely have been used as a floating fly with the ordinary rod and tackle of the dry-fly fisherman. The female is very much larger than the male. Candidly, I do not think the trout of the chalk streams take it well, except possibly after dark, and when the fly floating on the surface is invisible I have always held that it is time for the dry-fly sportsman to wind up and return to his home.

There now remain for consideration the large number of Caddis-flies which are found during the summer and autumn. From, say, the second week in June they are plentiful, and are taken freely by trout and grayling of all sizes, even including the very largest. As a rule this type of fly is visible to the fish, when, to quote my own words in " Dry Fly Entomology," 2nd edition, page 88, " enveloped in a thin pupal skin, it floats up through the water, or crawls along stones or weeds until it finds a convenient place for effecting the next and last change," to that of the imago or perfect insect. They are also visible to the fish when the imagines return to the water to lay their eggs, at which stage some descend under the surface to select a favourable spot, while some deposit the egg mass on leaves or stems of water-plants, and others fluttering on the surface drop their eggs, which sink to the bed of the river and adhere to the stones.

Oviposition, especially during the hottest weather, usually occurs at or just after dusk, but early in the summer or in the late autumn the Trichoptera will often be seen during the afternoon busily engaged in carrying out this, the most important part of their life's work, perpetuation of the species. Whenever and wherever these Caddis-flies are on the water, the trout and grayling are likely to feed on them and be tempted by a good imitation. After collecting a great number and classifying them as to size and colour, it was evident that, in addition to the welshman's button and large red sedge, the remaining genera and species of Trichoptera, although very numerous, could be fairly represented by a compromise which I decided to effect so as not to encumber the series with a very large number of patterns, all very similar in colour, shape, and size, and accordingly I worked them out in three colour schemes. Each of these colour schemes no doubt comprises a considerable number of genera and species of British Trichoptera, but the most critical observer would probably admit that, for the short sedge fly rise and the failing light generally prevailing at the time of its occurrence, these three patterns are amply sufficient.

No. 31, a distinctly dark-coloured fly of a dusky

brown hue, is called for convenience a small dark sedge, and is dressed on a No. 1 hook. No. 32, paler, slightly more ruddy, and larger, is called the medium sedge, and is dressed on a No. 2 hook. No. 33, the largest of these sedges, represents a fly which has mottled wings of a cinnamon tint, the ventral side of the body is a dull yellow-green, and the legs and antennæ are brown ginger ; it is dressed on a No. 3 hook, and is called the cinnamon sedge. After dressing the patterns I identified the natural insects with which they had been matched, and, to obviate the possibility of error, asked one of the first entomologists of the day to name them independently. The little dark sedge was a male *Goera pilosa*, the medium sedge a female of the same species, and the cinnamon sedge a male *Limnophilus lunatus*.

The foregoing are the 33 patterns comprised in the series, and when they had all been exhaustively tried and finally adopted, I thought it desirable to keep correct examples for future reference. With this view, and in order to give fishermen an opportunity of seeing them and possibly comparing flies they had bought with authentic copies of the originals, I suggested to two of the leading tackle-makers in this country, Messrs. C. Farlow & Co. and Messrs. Hardy Brothers, that they should each dress a correct set of these new patterns. This work was most satisfactorily carried out, and the two sets of flies, appropriately mounted, named, signed, and enclosed

in strong serviceable cases, were presented to the
Fly Fishers' Club. They are always available for
members of the club, and a non-member could no
doubt persuade a member friend to introduce him
to the room if the necessity for making a comparison
should arise.

CHAPTER IV

THE PATTERNS AND THEIR DRESSINGS

Illustrated by nine coloured plates of the artificial flies

I WILL not apologise for beginning this chapter with a further reference to the colour question, because the *raison d'être* of this book is, after all, an attempt to reproduce in the artificial flies the exact shades and tones of colour of the natural insects they are intended to counterfeit. The absence of a recognised scientific colour nomenclature has often been deplored by practical men in the past, as tending to increase the difficulty of describing shades and tones of colour in words which would convey to scientific men all over the world the same idea To talk of the various shades of what fly fishermen generally call *olive* as green olive, brown olive, pale and dark, smoky and dusky olive, will not bring home to the reader any very definite notion of what is intended by the particular words used in a particular case.

An attempt has been made in recent years to establish an exhaustive colour chart, and in the opinion of many this has at last been eminently successful. The Royal Horticultural Society has brought promi-

nently before the British public the colour chart
published in 1905 under the following title :—

" RÉPERTOIRE DE COULEURS *pour aider à la déter-
mination des couleurs* DES FLEURS, DES FEUILLAGES
ET DES FRUITS, *publié par la* SOCIÉTÉ FRANÇAISE DES
CHRYSANTHÉMISTES *et* RENÉ OBERTHUR, *avec la colla-
boration principale de* HENRI DAUTHENAY *et celle
de MM. Julien Mouillefert, C. Harman Payne, Max
Leichtlin, N. Severi et Miguel Cortés.*"

Although primarily intended to be a guide to
aid in the determination of the colours of flowers,
foliage, and fruit, it is a full and exhaustive chart
of colours of all sorts. It contains 365 sheets, num-
bered consecutively, each of one colour, in four distinct shades, arranged in the following order : white,
yellow, orange, red, rose, purple, violet, blue, green,
brown, maroon, black, and grey. There are no less
than 38 different tones of yellow, 62 of green, 34
of brown, and 13 of maroon, each, as before remarked,
in four distinct shades. These are referred to specifi-
cally because they comprise all the colours of dyed
materials used in dressing the set of patterns, and
after devoting many days to the work I have succeeded in matching from eighteen pages of the chart
every one of the colours. These, by permission of
the publishers, I have been allowed to reproduce in
this book.

Every fly-dresser, whether of salmon or trout flies,
should welcome the appearance of such a chart as
containing every colour required for his work, and,

what is even of greater importance, establishing a
means of conveying to his work-hands, or to his
customer, a clear indication of what the colour called
by a specific name is understood to be, and in addition giving means of matching colours without seeing
the pattern itself. It constitutes, in fact, a serious
and generally successful attempt to devise that great
desideratum, a more or less scientific system of colour
nomenclature.

To criticise verbal descriptions of colours is not
a difficult matter, and no doubt a carping critic could
in some instances find fault with the names given.
A serious attempt, however, on the part of the said
carping critic to find correct and appropriate appella-
tions for hundreds of tints such as are given in the
chart would convince him of the insuperable difficulty
of such a task.

Some humorist, I think in *Punch*, produced a
cartoon of a Cabinet meeting summoned to discuss
some very important and imminent political question.
At the termination of a long discussion, the then
Premier was depicted as expressing to the other
members of the Cabinet his conclusions in something like the following terms · "It really does not
matter much what we say on the subject, so long
as we all say the same thing." As an inducement
to my brother anglers to adopt the nomenclature
of the Royal Horticultural Society's colour chart,
I would somewhat parody this sentiment by sug-
gesting that *it really does not matter much what*

PLATE I

MAY FLIES

NO I
GREEN MAY FLY
MALE

NO 2
GREEN MAY FLY
FEMALE

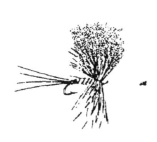

NO 3
BROWN MAY FLY
MALE

NO 4
BROWN MAY FLY
FEMALE

FLIES DRESSED BY MESSRS HARDY BROS LTD ALNWICK AND 61 PALL MALL LONDON S W

their imagines, the sherry spinners, on o hooks. The fly-dresser will do well to select the shortest hooks of the size specified for the males, and the longest for the females.

The following is the full list of the series of patterns, with details of dressing, for the use of the practical fly-tyer :—

No. 1.—GREEN MAYFLY (MALE)

(Illustrated in Plate I.)

Wings.—Rouen Drake dyed a bright greenish grey—*Glauque grisâtre* (246, shade 3)

Head Hackle.—Hen Golden Pheasant, taken from neck

Shoulder Hackles.—Two cock hackles dyed a medium shade of Naples yellow—*Jaune de Naples* (29, shade 3)

Body—Undyed Rofia grass with five turns of pale madder brown —*Brun de garance*—horsehair (334, shade 1), worked close together at the tail end, and this horsehair carried up the body to the shoulder in four open turns or ribs

Whisk.—Gallina dyed a very dark chocolate brown—*Brun Caroube* (342, shade 4)

Hook.—No 2.

No 2.—GREEN MAYFLY (FEMALE)

(Illustrated in Plate I.)

Wings.—Mallard dyed to shade a pale grey green—*Glauque d'Œillet* (247, shade 3).

Head Hackle.—Hen Golden Pheasant, taken from neck.

Shoulder Hackles—Two pale cream cock hackles.

Body.—Undyed Rofia grass with six close turns at tail end, and five turns ribbing body of medium cinnamon—*Cannelle*— horsehair (323, shade 3)

Whisk—Gallina dyed a very dark chocolate brown (342, shade 4).

Hook.—No. 3.

C

No 3 —BROWN MAYFLY (MALE)

(*Illustrated in Plate I*)

Wings.—Rouen Drake dyed snuff brown—*Brun Havane* (303, shade 2)

Head Hackle —Grey Hen.

Shoulder Hackles —Two sandy ginger cock hackles.

Body —Undyed Rofia grass with five close turns at tail end, and four turns ribbing body of very dark chocolate brown horsehair (342, shade 4).

Whisk.—Gallina dyed very dark chocolate brown (342, shade 4).

Hook —No. 2

No 4.—BROWN MAYFLY (FEMALE)

(*Illustrated in Plate I.*)

Wings.—Rouen Drake dyed golden bronze green—*Bronze de Médaille* (298, shade 2).

Head Hackle.—Brown Partridge.

Shoulder Hackles.—Two pale ginger cock hackles.

Body.—Undyed Rofia grass with six close turns at tail end, and five turns ribbing body of pale madder brown (334, shade 1) horsehair.

Whisk.—Gallina dyed very dark chocolate brown (342, shade 4).

Hook —No. 3

No. 5 —SPENT GNAT (MALE)

(*Illustrated in Plate II*)

Wings —Four dark Andalusian cock hackles set on horizontally.

Head Hackle.—Dark Grouse.

Shoulder Hackles.—Two cock hackles dyed a pale shade of Naples yellow—*Jaune de Naples* (29, shade 2).

Body.—Undyed Rofia grass with six close turns at tail end, and five turns ribbing body of very dark chocolate brown horsehair (342, shade 4)

Whisk —Gallina dyed a very dark chocolate brown (342, shade 4).

Hook.—No 3

PLATE 11
SPENT GNATS

No. 5
SPENT GNAT, MALE

No. 6
SPENT GNAT, FEMALE

FLIES DRESSED BY C. FARLOW & Co., LTD., LONDON.
(10, CHARLES STREET, ST JAMES'S SQUARE, S.W. AND 191, STRAND, W.C.)

PLATE III

OLIVE DUNS

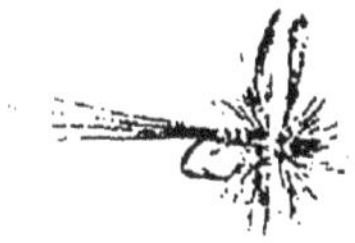

No 7
OLIVE DUN
MALE

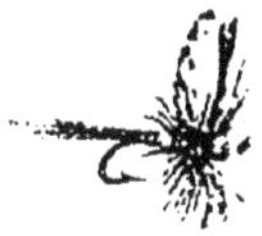

No 8
OLIVE DUN
FEMALE

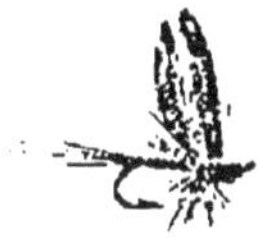

No 9
DARK OLIVE DUN
MALE

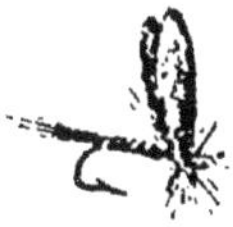

No 10
DARK OLIVE DUN
FEMALE

FLIES DRESSED BY MESSRS HARDY BROS LTD ALNWICK AND 61 PALL MALL LONDON S W

No. 6 —SPENT GNAT (FEMALE)

(Illustrated in Plate II)

Wings.—Four medium Andalusian cock hackles set on horizontally.
Hackles.—Two pale Andalusian cock hackles.
Body.—Rofia grass dyed pale yellow ochre—*Ocre Jaune* (326, shade 1)—with two close turns at tail end, and six turns ribbing body of condor quill dyed very dark chocolate brown (342, shade 4)
Whisk—Gallina dyed very dark chocolate brown (342, shade 4).
Hook.—No. 3, long.

No. 7 —OLIVE DUN (MALE)

(Illustrated in Plate III.)

Wings.—Medium starling.
Hackles.—Two cock hackles dyed golden bronze green (298, shade 2).
Body.—Stripped condor dyed golden bronze green (298, shade 2).
Whisk.—Gallina dyed golden bronze green (298, shade 2)
Head.—Three close turns of pale maroon—*Marron*—horsehair (341, shade 1).
Hook.—No. 0

No. 8 —OLIVE DUN (FEMALE)

(Illustrated in Plate III)

Wings—Medium starling
Hackles—Two cock hackles dyed pale golden bronze green (298, shade 1)
Body—Three close turns of stripped condor dyed primrose yellow—*Jaune primevère* (19, shade 1)—at tail end, and remainder of body of stripped condor dyed pale golden bronze green (298, shade 1)
Whisk.—Gallina dyed pale golden bronze green (298, shade 1)
Hook—No 0

N B—The female olive dun is a shade paler than the male in wings, hackles, body, and whisk.

No. 9 —DARK OLIVE DUN (MALE)

(Illustrated in Plate III)

Wings —Coot

Hackles —Two cock hackles dyed old olive green—*Olive passée* (299, shade 2)

Body —Stripped condor dyed old olive green (299, shade 2)

Whisk —Gallina dyed old olive green (299, shade 2)

Head—Three close turns of horsehair dyed dark Van Dyck brown —*Brun Van Dyck* (340, shade 4)

Hook —No 0

No 10 —DARK OLIVE DUN (FEMALE)

(Illustrated in Plate III)

Wings.—Coot

Hackles —Two cock hackles dyed pale old olive green (299, shade 1)

Body —Stripped condor dyed pale old olive green (299, shade 1).

Whisk.—Gallina dyed pale old olive green (299, shade 1).

Hook —No 0

No 11 —OLIVE SPINNER (MALE)

(Illustrated in Plate IV)

Wings —Two medium blue dun cock hackles set on horizontally.

Hackle —A cock hackle dyed dark putty colour—*Mastic* (311, shade 4).

Body —At tail end three close turns of horsehair dyed dark Van Dyck brown (340, shade 4), then twelve close turns horsehair dyed dull yellow green—*Vert Pyrite* (292, shade 3)—and at thorax four close turns horsehair dyed dark maroon (341, shade 4).

Whisk —Gallina dyed dark putty colour (311, shade 4)

Head.—Three close turns of horsehair dyed dark Van Dyck brown (340, shade 4)

Hook.—No. 0.

Plate IV

OLIVE SPINNERS

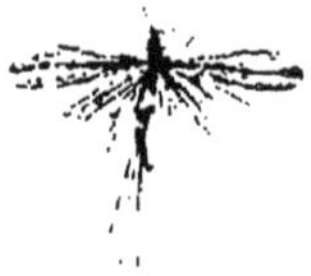

No 11
OLIVE SPINNER, MALE

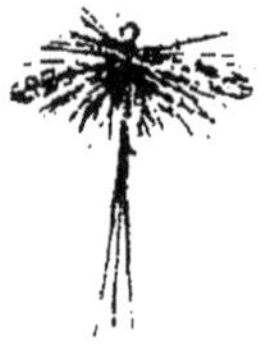

No 12
OLIVE SPINNER, FEMALE

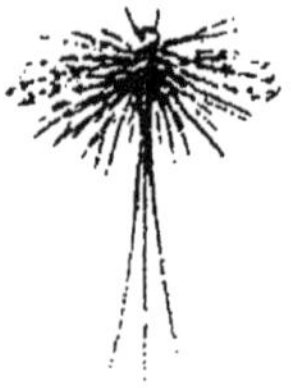

No 13
OLIVE (RED) SPINNER FEMALE

Flies Dressed by C Farlow & Co Ltd London
10 Charles Street St James's Square S W and 191 Strand W C

No 12 —OLIVE SPINNER (FEMALE)

(*Illustrated in Plate IV.*)

Wings.—Two medium blue dun cock hackles set on horizontally

Hackle —A cock hackle dyed golden bronze green (298, shade 2).

Body.—At tail end three close turns of stripped condor dyed primrose yellow (19, shade 1), and remainder of body of stripped condor dyed golden bronze green (298, shade 2)

Whisk —Gallina dyed golden bronze green (298, shade 2)

Hook —No o.

This is an imitation of the female olive spinner in the act of or immediately after oviposition

No 13.—OLIVE (RED) SPINNER (FEMALE)

(*Illustrated in Plate IV.*)

Wings.—Two medium grizzly blue dun cock hackles set on horizontally

Hackle —A cock hackle dyed pale golden bronze green (298, shade 1).

Body.—Stripped condor dyed dark dead leaf—*Feuille morte* (321, shade 4)

Whisk.—Gallina dyed pale golden bronze green (298, shade 1).

Hook —No o

This is an imitation of the female olive spinner when *spent—i e.* at the last stage after oviposition, when it falls almost lifeless on to the surface of the water.

No 14.—PALE WATERY DUN (MALE)

(*Illustrated in Plate V.*)

Wings.—Pale starling

Hackles —Two cock hackles dyed a full shade of Naples yellow—*Jaune de Naples* (29, shade 4)

Body.—Stripped condor dyed a full shade of sulphury white—*Blanc soufré* (14, shade 4).

Whisk—Gallina dyed a pale shade of Naples yellow (29, shade 4).

Head—Three close turns of horsehair dyed pale dead leaf colour (321, shade 1).

Hook—No. oo.

No. 15—PALE WATERY DUN (FEMALE)

(Illustrated in Plate V.)

Wings.—Pale starling.

Hackles—Two cock hackles dyed a medium shade of Naples yellow (29, shade 3).

Body.—Stripped condor dyed sulphury white (14, shade 3).

Whisk—Gallina dyed medium Naples yellow (29, shade 3).

Hook.—No. oo.

No. 16—PALE WATERY SPINNER (MALE)

(Illustrated in Plate V.)

Wings.—Two pale cream cock hackles set on horizontally.

Hackle.—A cock hackle dyed a full shade of Naples yellow (29, shade 4)

Body—At tail end three close turns of horsehair dyed dark dead leaf (321, shade 4), then nine close turns of white horsehair, and four close turns of chocolate-brown horsehair (342, shade 2) at shoulder.

Whisk—Gallina dyed a full shade of Naples yellow (29, shade 4).

Head.—Three close turns of horsehair dyed dark dead leaf (321, shade 4).

Hook.—No oo.

No. 17.—PALE WATERY SPINNER (FEMALE)

(Illustrated in Plate V)

Wings—Two cock hackles dyed a full shade of Naples yellow (29, shade 4), set on horizontally.

Hackle.—A cock hackle dyed a full shade of Naples yellow (29, shade 4).

PLATE V

PALE WATERY DUNS AND SPINNERS

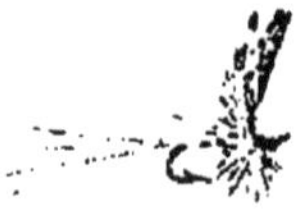

No 14
PALE WATERY DUN
MALE

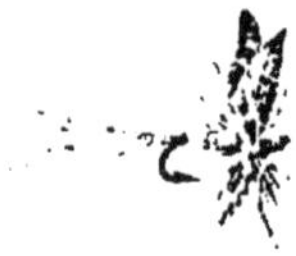

No 15
PALE WATERY DUN
FEMALE

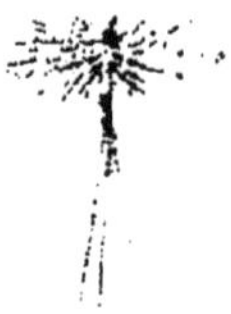

No 16
PALE WATERY SPINNER
MALE

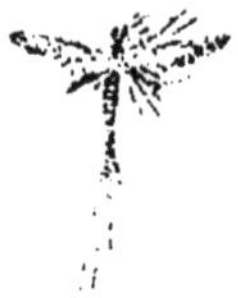

No 17
PALE WATERY SPINNER
FEMALE

FLIES DRESSED BY MESSRS HARDY BROS LTD ALNWICK AND 61 PALL MALL, LONDON S W

PLATE VI

IRON BLUE DUNS AND SPINNERS

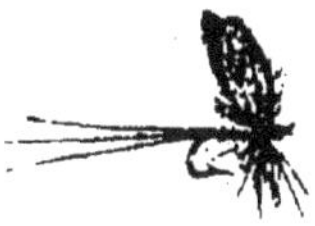

No 18
IRON BLUE DUN
MALE

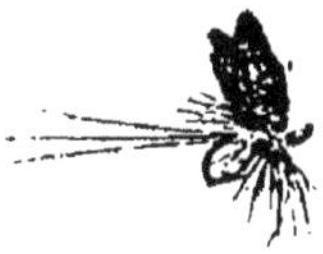

No 19
IRON BLUE DUN
FEMALE

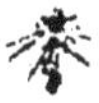

No 20
IRON BLUE SPINNER
MALE

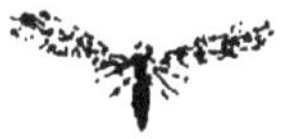

No 21
IRON BLUE SPINNER
FEMALE

FLIES DRESSED BY C FARLOW & CO LTD LONDON
10 CHARLES STREET ST JAMES'S SQUARE S W AND 191 STRAND W C

Body —Stripped condor dyed a full shade of Naples yellow (29, shade 4).

Whisk —Gallina dyed a very pale Naples yellow (29, shade 1).

Hook.—No. oo.

No 18.—IRON-BLUE DUN (MALE)

(*Illustrated in Plate VI*)

Wings —Dark starling dyed bluish black —*Noir bleuté* (348, shade 1)

Hackles —Two grizzly dun cock hackles

Body —Stripped condor dyed dark old olive green (299, shade 3).

Whisk —Gallina dyed dark old olive green (299, shade 3).

Head —Three close turns of horsehair dyed dark Van Dyck brown (340, shade 4).

Hook —No. oo

No. 19 —IRON-BLUE DUN (FEMALE)

(*Illustrated in Plate VI.*)

Wings.—Dark starling dyed bluish black (348, shade 1)

Hackles —Two cock hackles dyed pale golden bronze green (298, shade 1).

Body —Stripped condor dyed pale golden bronze green (298, shade 1).

Whisk.—Gallina dyed pale golden bronze green (298, shade 1)

Hook —No. oo.

No 20.—IRON-BLUE SPINNER (MALE)

(*Illustrated in Plate VI*)

Wings.—Two pale cream cock hackles set on horizontally.

Hackle —A pale cream cock hackle.

Body.—At tail end three close turns of horsehair dyed dark Van Dyck brown (340, shade 4), then nine close turns of white horsehair and four close turns of very dark chocolate-brown horsehair (342, shade 4) at thorax

Whisk.—Cream white gallina.

Head—Three close turns of dark Van Dyck brown horsehair (340, shade 4).
Hook.—No oo

This is the imitation of the well-known jenny spinner, the imago of the male iron-blue dun (*Bactis pumilus*).

No. 21 —IRON-BLUE SPINNER (FEMALE)

(*Illustrated in Plate VI*)

Wings —Two pale rusty dun cock hackles set on horizontally.
Hackle —A cream cock hackle
Body.—Stripped condor dyed dark maroon (341, shade 3), with four close turns of very dark chocolate-brown horsehair (342, shade 4) at thorax.
Whisk.—Cream white gallina.
Hook.—No oo

No 22.—BLUE-WINGED OLIVE (MALE)

(*Illustrated in Plate VII*)

Wings —Coot, rather dark.
Hackles —Two cock hackles dyed golden bronze green (298, shade 2)
Body —Stripped condor dyed golden bronze green (298, shade 2)
Whisk —Gallina dyed golden bronze green (298, shade 2).
Head —Three close turns of pale maroon horsehair (341, shade 1).
Hook —No o

No. 23 —BLUE-WINGED OLIVE (FEMALE)

(*Illustrated in Plate VII.*)

Wings.—Coot, medium.
Hackles.—Two cock hackles dyed pale golden bronze green (298, shade 1).

Plate VII

BLUE WINGED OLIVES AND SHERRY SPINNERS

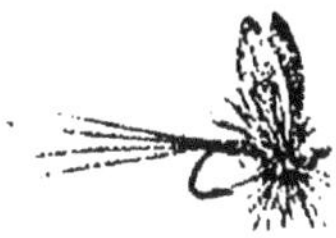

No 22
BLUE WINGED OLIVE
MALE

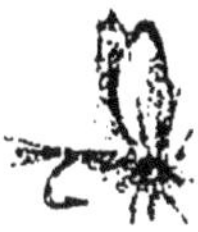

No 23
BLUE WINGED OLIVE
FEMALE

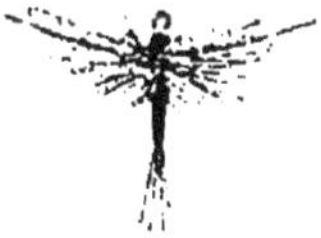

No 24
SHERRY SPINNER
MALE

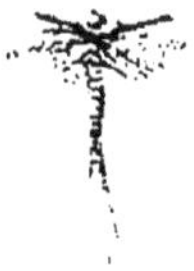

No 25
SHERRY SPINNER
FEMALE

Flies Dressed by Messrs Hardy Bros Ltd, Alnwick and 61 Pall Mall London S.W.

Body —Stripped condor dyed pale golden bronze green (298, shade 1).
Whisk.—Gallina dyed pale golden bronze green (298, shade 1).
Hook.—No o.

The blue-winged olive is proportionately a little longer in the wings than the olive dun, and therefore conveys the impression of being a larger insect than it really is

No 24.—SHERRY SPINNER (MALE)

(*Illustrated in Plate VII*)

Wings —Two grizzly blue dun cock hackles set on horizontally.
Hackle.—A cock hackle dyed pale golden bronze green (298, shade 1)
Body.—Stripped condor dyed dark madder brown (334, shade 4), ribbed with pale Van Dyck brown horsehair (340, shade 1), and four close turns of the same horsehair at shoulder.
Whisk.—Gallina dyed pale golden bronze green (298, shade 1)
Head.—Three close turns of pale maroon horsehair (341, shade 1)
Hook.—No o.

No. 25 —SHERRY SPINNER (FEMALE)

(*Illustrated in Plate VII*)

Wings.—Two pale-ginger cock hackles set on horizontally.
Hackle —A pale-ginger cock hackle.
Body —Stripped condor dyed pale cinnamon (323, shade 1)
Whisk —Gallina dyed pale cinnamon (323, shade 1).
Hook.—No o.

The female sherry spinner or imago of the blue-winged olive (*Ephemerella ignita*) lays a bunch of blue-green eggs, and the above pattern (which it will be noted is nearly self-coloured) is an imitation of it at the last stage after oviposition

No. 26.—BLACK GNAT (MALE)

(*Illustrated in Plate VIII.*)

Wings.—Two pale blue dun cock hackles.
Hackles —Two glossy black starling hackles.
Body —Undyed peacock quill with four close turns of black horse-
    hair at shoulder.
Head —Three close turns of pale maroon horsehair (341, shade 1).
Hook.—No oo

No 27.—BLACK GNAT (FEMALE)

(*Illustrated in Plate VIII.*)

Wings.—Pale starling
Hackles —Two glossy black starling hackles.
Body.—Peacock quill dyed jet-black
Hook.—No. oo

The black gnat of the angler is *Bibio johannis,* one of the
Diptera, and the imitations are the most successful modern patterns
for smutting fish

No. 28.—BROWN ANT

(*Illustrated in Plate VIII.*)

Wings —Pale starling
Hackles.—Two furnace cock hackles.
Body.—The knob at the tail end is made of unstripped condor
    dyed dark maroon (341, shade 3), and the remainder of the
    body of stripped condor dyed the same colour.
Hook.—No oo

No 29 —WELSHMAN'S BUTTON (MALE)

(*Illustrated in Plate VIII.*)

Wings.—Dark-brown hen or a lighter feather dyed pale maroon
    (341, shade 1)
Hackles.—Two furnace cock hackles.

Plate VIII

BLACK GNATS, BROWN ANT AND WELSHMAN'S BUTTON

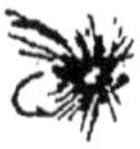

No 26
BLACK GNAT
MALE

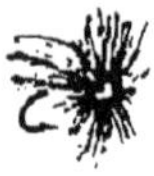

No 27
BLACK GNAT
FEMALE

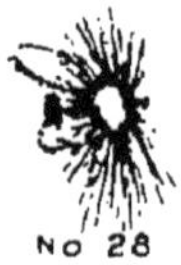

No 28
BROWN ANT

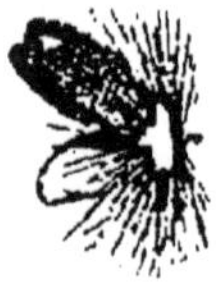

No 29
WELSHMANS BUTTON
MALE

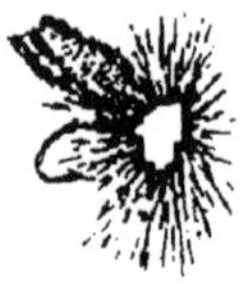

No 30
WELSHMANS BUTTON
FEMALE

Flies Dressed by C Farlow & Co Ltd London
10 Charles Street St James's Square S W and 191 Strand W C

Plate IX

SEDGES

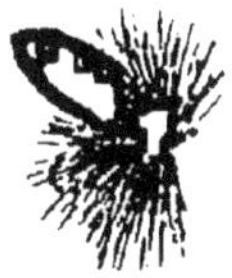

No 31
SMALL DARK SEDGE

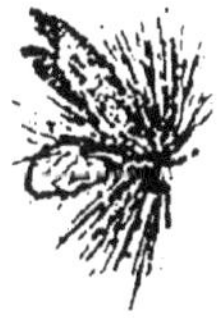

No 32
MEDIUM SEDGE

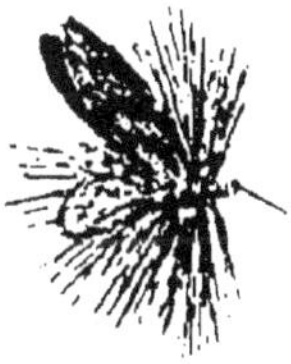

No 33
CINNAMON SEDGE

Flies Dressed by C Farlow & Co Ltd London
0 Charles Street St James's Square S W and 191 Strand W C

Body.—A thin strip torn from the central quill of a brown hen wing-feather dyed chocolate brown (342, shade 3) and worked with the glossy side outwards, ribbed with pale maroon horse-hair (341, shade 1).

Hook.—No. 2.

No. 30.—WELSHMAN'S BUTTON (FEMALE)

(*Illustrated in Plate VIII.*)

Wings.—Brown hen distinctly paler than the wings of the male.

Hackles.—Two furnace cock hackles

Body.—At tail end four close turns of unstripped condor dyed dark cinnamon (323, shade 4), and remainder of body a thin strip torn from the central quill of a brown hen wing-feather dyed dark chocolate brown (342, shade 3), worked with the glossy side outwards and ribbed with pale maroon horsehair (341, shade 1).

Hook.—No 3.

No 31.—SMALL DARK SEDGE

(*Illustrated in Plate IX.*)

Wings —Landrail dyed dark chocolate brown (342, shade 3)

Hackles.—Two dark furnace cock hackles.

Ribbing Hackle.—A dark furnace cock hackle

Body.—Stripped condor dyed very dark maroon (341, shade 4)

Hook —No 1.

No. 32 —MEDIUM SEDGE

(*Illustrated in Plate IX.*)

Wings.—Landrail, selecting full-coloured feathers

Hackles.—Two ginger cock hackles.

Ribbing Hackle.—A ginger cock hackle

Body.—Unstripped condor dyed medium cinnamon (323, shade 3).

Hook.—No. 2

No. 33 —CINNAMON SEDGE

(Illustrated in Plate IX.)

Wings.—Mottled brown hen, selecting well-marked feathers.
Hackles.—Two ginger cock hackles
Ribbing Hackle —A ginger cock hackle.
Body —Stripped condor dyed dull yellow-green (292, shade 4).
Hook.—No. 3

CHAPTER V

TOOLS AND MATERIALS REQUIRED

THE modern fly-dresser does not require a large number of tools, and they are not of a very costly nature. There are possibly left some of the old school who hold the hook between the thumb and forefinger of the left hand, and with the exception of some little assistance rendered by the other fingers of that hand, do all the work with the right hand. With every respect for their superior deftness, one cannot help feeling some pity for them, and possibly wonder why they have not adopted the manifest improvement of a vice firmly fixed to the table, and holding the hook rigidly in position so as to enable them to use both hands in tying the fly.

The old pattern of vice made by Messrs. Holtz-apffel for the writer is quite practical, but the form designed by the late Mr. Hawksley and called by his name, which is also made by Messrs. Holtz-apffel, is a great improvement on it. I am, however, decidedly of opinion that the Thompson vice, an American invention lately seen in this country, is the most convenient of all.

I append a description of it, thanks to the kind

assistance of Mr. Martin E. Mosely, and give a drawing showing its form and construction in Fig. 1.

"The Thompson Fly-tying Vice

"To the majority of amateur fly-dressers, the Thompson fly-tying vice is probably quite unknown. Described by Mr. Charles C. Elliott in an American periodical, this extremely handy tool has only recently made its way over to this country. Its originality of design might conceivably cause it to be looked upon with some suspicion, but its construction has been well thought out, and the inventor appears to have overcome all the faults and objectionable features which are inherent in the ordinary cheap vice, obtained for a shilling or so at the tackle shop.

A Thompson vice which I have had in constant use for some time has proved absolutely reliable, and the jaws show no sign of having been dented or in any way forced out of shape by the hook.

Apart from the mechanism of the instrument, the most original feature is undoubtedly the upturned handle of the cam which operates the jaws. This handle forms a rest for the left hand, and steadying it, greatly augments the comfort and pleasure of fly-tying.

It will be noted that in use there is a continual tendency of the jaws to grip the hook more firmly, as the weight of the hand automatically works the cam.

The vice has another feature which it shares in common with the Hawksley vice, namely, the projecting jaws, which are so arranged that the hook stands out well away from the standard, thus allowing plenty of room for manipulation. In tying horsehair-bodied spinners when three hackle pliers are hanging down simultaneously, this feature will be specially appreciated, as with the ordinary pattern of vice the strands of horsehair are apt to get twisted together, causing much con-fusion and loss of time and patience.

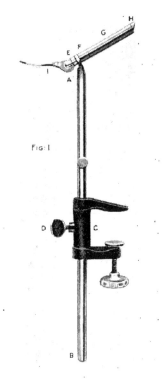

FIG. I

In the original pattern, a brass rod is passed through the standard at right angles to it, and secured in position by a screw. At the extre-mity of the rod there is a rubber washer held against a metal disc by a small nut. This rod can be adjusted by sliding it backwards and for-wards to clip the tying silk at any distance from the standard that the operator may desire. Personally I have discarded this clip, as I found that the securing taut of the tying silk was an embarrassment and resulted in frequent breakages and much consequent loss of time. In practice, as Mr. Halford subsequently observes, if the silk is sufficiently waxed, neither clip nor hackle pliers will be found necessary.

In the accompanying sketch, A B is the standard passing through a clamp C and adjusted to a con-venient height above the table by the screw D. E,

F, and G are three lengths of hollow tubing through which is passed a split chuck H, which is shaped to take the hook. I is the cam fixed to the extremity of the chuck by a pin.

It will be seen that when the handle of the cam is depressed a strong leverage is exerted against the section of tubing E, with the result that the chuck is drawn through the tubing until the pressure of the edge of the tube G against the shoulder of the jaws causes them to close. The action of the jaws is as nearly as possible parallel, and the maximum of gripping power is thus obtained.

MARTIN E. MOSELY."

The form of the jaws of this vice is most convenient, and the lever on the left-hand side of the cam operating the jaws is an admirable rest for the left hand during the operations of tying the fly. The device of the late H. G. McClelland ("Athenian" of the *Fishing Gazette*) for holding the tying silk taut at any stage of the manipulation is fitted to this form of vice, and, for those who require this aid, is no doubt a handy arrangement. Personally, I find that with well-waxed silk there is no need to secure the end of the tying silk, and I have often put away in a drawer a partially dressed fly with the tying silk loose, and left it for many days until I could resume the work, to find everything in position just as I had left it.

The hackle pliers in the form shown in Fig. 2 are absolutely essential, and it is useful to have at least three pairs of them when dressing the patterns of spinners with horsehair bodies.

A pair of curved oculist's scissors, a blunt needle fixed in a short handle, a pair of fine-pointed curved pliers to pick up feathers or any other small objects used in the work, and a very short or stiff tooth-brush to brush the hackles, &c., into position when the fly is completed, are all the tools that are really necessary. An ordinary white porcelain photographic developing dish on the working table is useful to keep the hackles and other materials selected for the pattern together, and another advantage of it is that a sudden gust of wind from an open door or window will not scatter the feathers or blow them away.

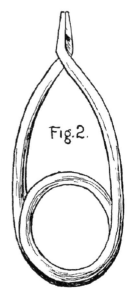

Fig. 2.

An electrical lamp, such as is described in "Dry Fly Entomology," is useful when working at night, but if the amateur thinks it too costly a luxury he can find many forms of candle lamps suitable for the purpose. In selecting one he should bear in mind that the light must be sufficient to illuminate the object from a point far enough from it to leave room for his fingers when tying the fly. The light should be reflected on to the object, and, unless he wishes to try his sight unnecessarily, the source of light itself must be invisible when

D

his head is in the position adopted by him when working.

With reference to the materials to be used in dressing the flies, the first and most important item is the hook, which is at once the foundation of the fly itself and the means of achieving the primary object of the angler in making an attachment to the fish when it rises to the artificial fly. To discuss the question of flies on eyed hooks *v.* flies on gut, or turned-up eyes *v.* turned-down eyes, should not be necessary, as in this twentieth century the eyed hook with upturned eye is firmly established as *the* form to be preferred by the dry-fly tyer and the dry-fly fisherman.

Pearsall's gossamer silk made for the purpose has been for the last quarter of a century, and is to-day, the very best fly-dressing silk on the market. Rod-makers' wax pulled out to make it lighter in colour, or one of the many sorts of white or transparent wax supplied by the tackle-makers, should be used to wax the silk, and a small bottle of shellac varnish is required to varnish the head of a fly when it is finished. The professional fly-dresser often neglects this process, and his carelessness in this respect is one of the reasons why the amateur's flies generally last longer in use than those bought from the shops or dressed by the trade. A constant source of irritation to the dry-fly fisherman is also the neglect of the fly-tyer to clear the eye of the hook of surplus varnish.

In working out the dressing of this series of

patterns, I kept steadfastly before me the desire of simplifying in every possible way the work and removing as far as possible one of the troubles of the old-fashioned fly-dresser—the enormous number of materials required to dress his flies correctly and to pattern. Silks in innumerable colours, dubbing or fur from a great variety of animals, crewels and other wools, tinsels, gold and silver, flat, in varying widths, wire or twist of various diameters, straw, india-rubber, and a host of other materials, had to be kept in the collection for making the bodies of the flies, while in the present series Rofia grass, condor quill, peacock quill, horsehair, and quill stripped from a brown hen wing-feather are all the body materials required. It has been a source of deep gratification to me that, with the exception of the hackle, there is no material used in this series which is either difficult or costly to obtain.

The hackles which are used to represent the flat wings of the spent gnats and spinners, the legs of the insect, and in some cases also carried down the body in open turns or ribs to assist in floating the pattern, have now to be considered. The difficulty of obtaining cock hackles of good shape, and taken from birds of the right age so as to be glossy and yet not too stiff, is the bane of the amateur's existence. He can pick up a few in the poulterer's shop, he can occasionally find some in distant country farmyards, and he can either breed the fowls himself or get a friend to do it for him. In almost every case it means endless trouble and disappointment, and considerable expense, and I fear that I can give him no very useful hints on the subject. The best advice to tender is that whenever and wherever he can secure good hackles he should purchase them in considerable numbers, and keep them for future use. He will require dun hackles of many descriptions, from the palest blue dun to the darkest Andalusian, and such varieties as grizzled, rusty, and other shades among the duns, also ginger in many shades, furnace light and dark, white or cream-coloured for dyeing, and starling hackles for the black gnats.

Close-plumed feathers are used as hackles for some of the patterns, comprising the hen golden pheasant, grey hen, brown partridge, and grouse. To prepare a close-plumed feather for use as a hackle, the downy part at the root end must be stripped from the quill, and taking the extreme point between the left thumb and forefinger, the whole of the plume except the part held by the left thumb and forefinger should be stroked back by the right thumb and forefinger slightly moistened. The feather will then appear as shown in Fig. 3.

Fig. 3.

For wings of the mayflies, breast feathers from the Rouen drake and mallard are required, and for the remaining patterns, except the spinners and male black gnat (the wings of which are made of cock hackles), starling, coot, and brown hen wing-feathers are used. The first pinion feather of most birds is too stiff for use as wings, but the second, third, and fourth primaries are generally the best.

Rofia grass, which is used for bodies of mayflies and spent gnats, can be obtained from all nurserymen, and splits easily into strips of suitable width. Condor quill, which is the plume of wing or tail feathers, is the strongest and best material known for the bodies of the majority of patterns in the series. It should be noted that each plume (a single one of which should be used) has two flues on it, one much longer than the other. For some patterns the unstripped condor is used, but in the great majority it has to be stripped, i.e. both flues removed, and a smooth, slightly tapered flat quill left. To do this, lay a few strands as torn from the feather flat on the working table, and holding them securely by the points, draw the edge of a blunt knife towards the root end several times in succession until the whole of both plumes has been removed. After a little practice it will be found comparatively easy to do this.

Peacock quills, or strands from the eye feather of the peacock which are used in some cases, can be stripped of their metallic flue in the same way. They are far easier to strip, but the quill is not nearly so tough and strong, and condor should be invariably preferred to the weaker peacock quill.

The central quill from the brown hen feather
is removed by making an incision with a sharp
knife near the point of the feather, just raising the
quill and tearing it off. If there is any of the pith
adhering to the inner side of the quill, this should
also be removed with a blunt knife.

For the bodies of some of the male spinners,
for ribbing other bodies, and for the heads of the
male duns, spinners and black gnat, horsehair, white,
black, or dyed, is used. Purchase two or three hanks
as used for a violin bow, and you will find the horsehair is fairly straight, of uniform substance, and pale
or white in colour. In preparation it is probably
subjected to some treatment which removes much
of the natural grease, and this is a great boon if it
has to be dyed.

The only material left for consideration now is
that to be used for the whisk, as the tail or *setæ* of
the Ephemeridæ is generally called. Many years
ago the late G. S. Marryat recommended Gallina,
and in my humble opinion it is to-day the only
feather fit for making the whisk of a floating fly;
no other feather is at once so tough, stands so much
use, and is in substance and appearance so similar
to the setæ of the natural insect.

Many of the materials used have to be dyed, and
in some cases where they are too dark in natural
tone bleaching may be resorted to, either to get the
colour required or as a preliminary to dyeing to
the correct shade. For bleaching feathers, hydrogen

peroxide is used, and its action is accelerated by the addition of a few drops of liquid ammonia.

In reference to the processes of dyeing, there is practically nothing to add to the full instructions given in " Dry Fly Entomology," pages 230 to 238 in the 2nd edition. I must warn the amateur, however, that in no part of his work will he meet with more difficulty and disappointment than in the various processes of attempting to dye his materials to the correct colour and shade. The work of dyeing as carried on by the dyeing trade, in a factory specially designed and arranged for the work, supplied with the most modern appliances and machinery, and with skilled workmen trained to the work, is to some degree a series of experiments, and with all those advantages some of our fair friends of the gentler sex can tell us of innumerable cases where the precise shade and tint required could not be obtained.

It should be of great advantage to both amateurs and professionals to have a standard of colours and shades required for their dyed materials, and I have therefore appended (by kind permission of the publishers) the eighteen plates of colours on the chart of the Société Française des Chrysanthémistes, by means of which the colours of all the parts of the patterns requiring dyeing have been matched. These are given in Plates Nos. X. to XXVII. inclusive, and the page number of the original French colour chart is also given. There are four shades of each colour, and at the side of each shade the number of the pattern and parts to be dyed to the particular shade are given. They are as follows :—

Plate Number.	Page on Colour Chart.	English Name on Colour Chart.
X.	14	Sulphury White.
XI.	19	Primrose Yellow.
XII.	29	Naples Yellow.
XIII.	246	Bright Greenish Grey.
XIV.	247	Pale Grey Green.
XV.	292	Dull Yellow Green.
XVI.	298	Golden Bronze Green.
XVII.	299	Old Olive Green.
XVIII.	303	Snuff Brown.
XIX.	311	Putty Colour.
XX.	321	Dead Leaf.
XXI.	323	Cinnamon.
XXII.	326	Yellow Ochre.
XXIII.	334	Madder Brown.
XXIV.	340	Van Dyck Brown.
XXV.	341	Maroon.
XXVI.	342	Dark Chocolate Brown.
XXVII.	348	Bluish Black.

PLATE X

Sulphury White

Page 14 on Colour Chart

Patterns in which materials dyed to the various shades of this colour are used.

Shade	Pattern Number	Parts of Fly dyed to shade
1		
2		
3	15	Body.
4	14	Body.

1

2

3

4

PLATE XI

Primrose Yellow

Page 19 on Colour Chart

Patterns in which materials dyed to the various shades of this colour are used.

Shade	Pattern Number	Parts of Fly dyed to shade
1	8	Condor quill at tail end of body.
	12	,, ,,
2		
3		
4		

Naples Yellow

Page 29 on Colour Chart

Patterns in which materials dyed to the various shades of this colour are used.

Shade	Pattern Number	Parts of Fly dyed to shade
1	17	Whisk.
2	5	Shoulder hackles.
3	1	Shoulder hackles.
	15	Hackles & whisk.
4	14	Hackles & whisk.
	16	Hackle & whisk.
	17	Wings, hackle & body.

PLATE XIII

Bright Greenish Grey

Page 246 on Colour Chart

Patterns in which materials dyed to the various shades of this colour are used.

Shade	Pattern Number		Parts of Fly dyed to shade
1	1		
2	2		
3	3	I	Wings.
4	4		

PLATE XIV

Pale Grey Green

Page 247 on Colour Chart

Patterns in which materials dyed to the various shades of this colour are used.

Shade	Pattern Number	Parts of Fly dyed to shade
1	1	
2	2	
3	3	2	Wings.
4	4	

PLATE XV

Dull Yellow Green

Page 292 on Colour Chart

Patterns in which materials dyed to the various shades of this colour are used.

1 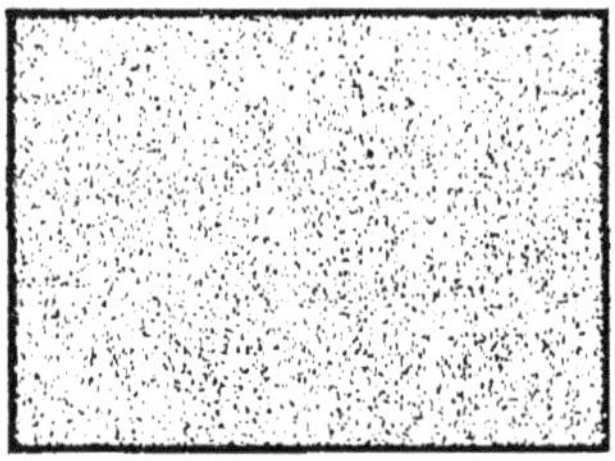

2 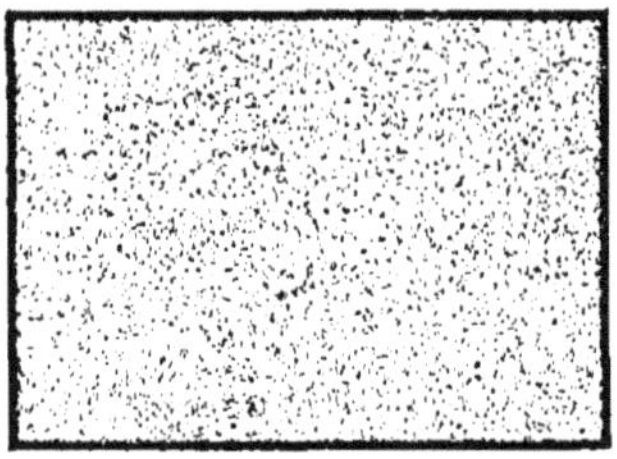

3 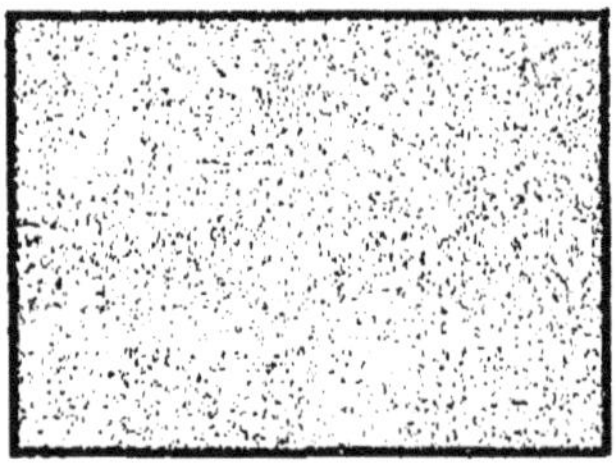

4 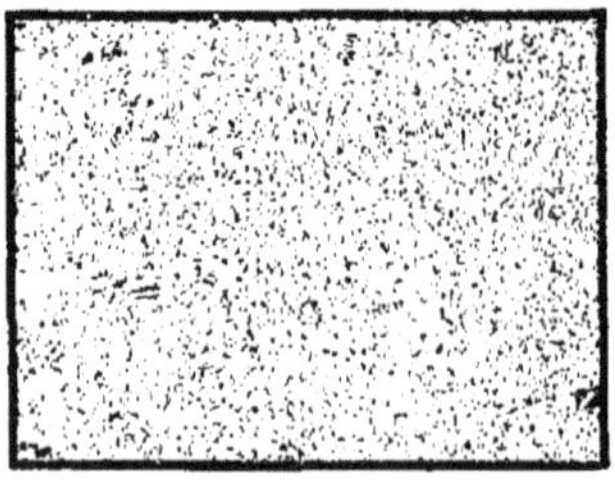

Shade	Pattern Number	Parts of Fly dyed to shade
1		
2		
3	11	Horsehair in middle of body.
4	33	Body.

PLATE XVI

Golden Bronze Green

Page 298 on Colour Chart

Patterns in which materials dyed to the various shades of this colour are used.

1 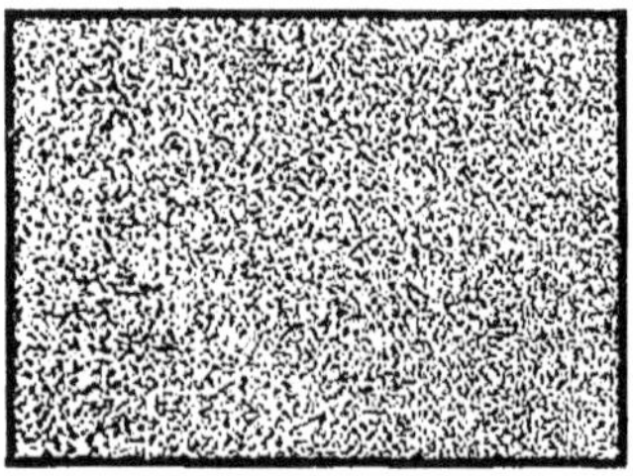

2 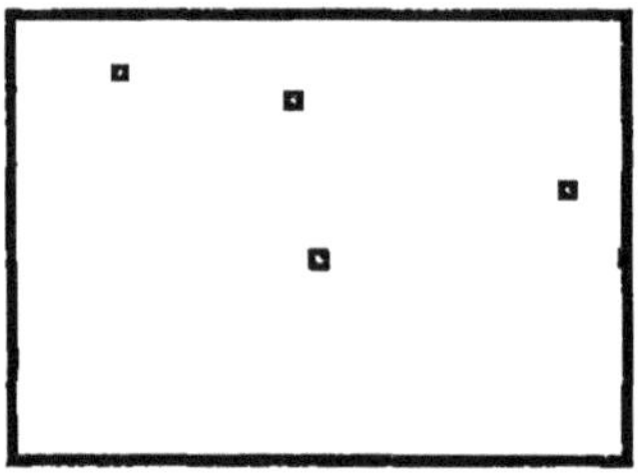

3

4

Shade	Pattern Number	Parts of Fly dyed to shade
1	8	Hackles, body & whisk.
	13	Hackle & whisk.
	19	Hackles, body & whisk.
	23	Hackles, body & whisk.
	24	Hackle & whisk.
2	4	Wings.
	7	Hackles, body & whisk.
	12	Hackle, body & whisk.
	22	Hackles, body & whisk.
3		
4		

PLATE XVII

Old Olive Green

Page 299 on Colour Chart

Patterns in which materials dyed to the various shades of this colour are used.

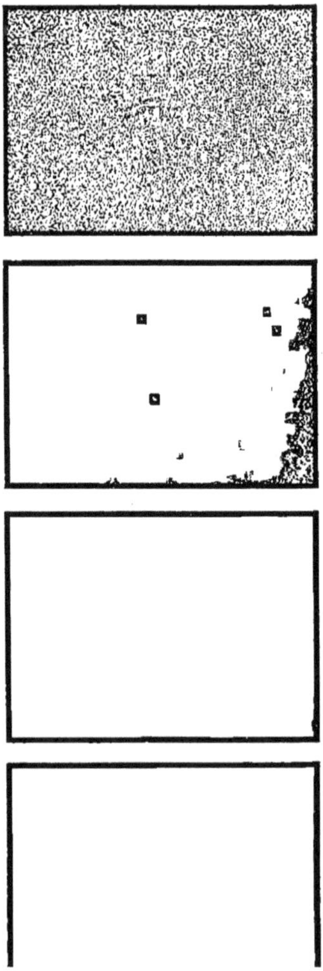

	Shade	Pattern Number	Parts of Fly dyed to shade
1	1	10	Hackles, body & whisk.
2	2	9	Hackles, body & whisk.
3	3	18	Body & whisk.
4	4		

PLATE XVIII

Snuff Brown

Page 303 on Colour Chart

Patterns in which materials dyed to the various shades of this colour are used.

1

2

3

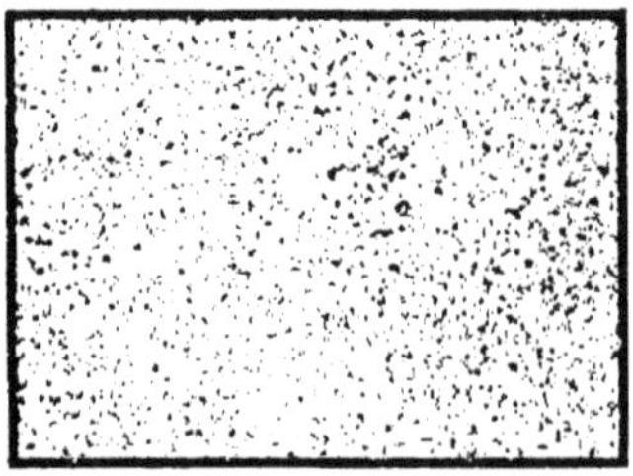

4

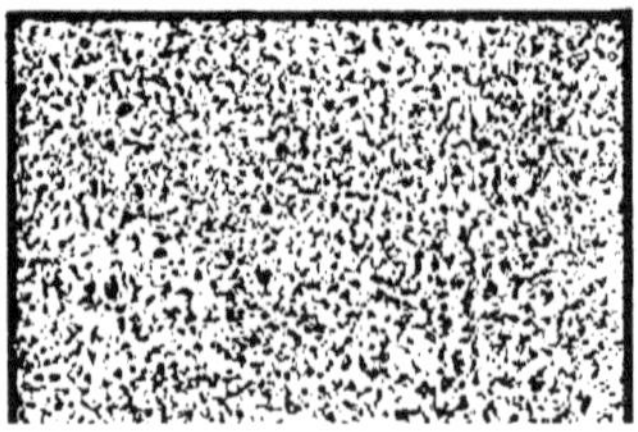

Shade	Pattern Number	Parts of Fly dyed to shade
1		
2	3	Wings.
3		
4		

PLATE XIX

Putty Colour

Page 311 on Colour Chart

Patterns in which materials dyed to the various shades of this colour are used.

Shade	Pattern Number	Parts of Fly dyed to shade
1		
2		
3		
4	11	Hackle & whisk.

PLATE XX

Dead Leaf

Page 321 on Colour Chart

Patterns in which materials dyed to the various shades of this colour are used.

	Shade	Pattern Number	Parts of Fly dyed to shade
1	1	14	Horsehair for head.
2	2		
3 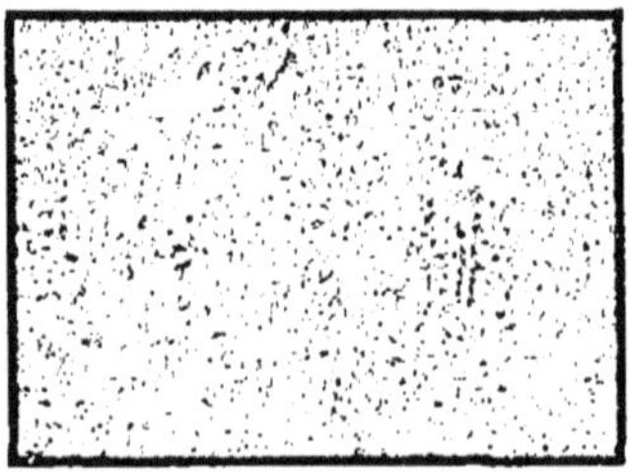	3		
4 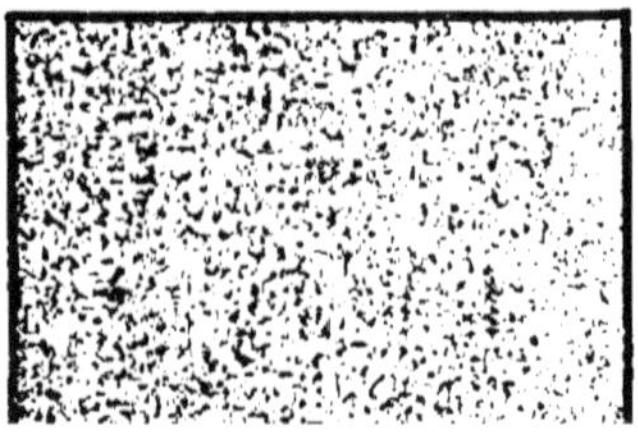	4	13 16	Body. Horsehair at tail end of body & head.

PLATE XXI

Cinnamon

Page 323 on Colour Chart

Patterns in which materials dyed to the various shades of this colour are used.

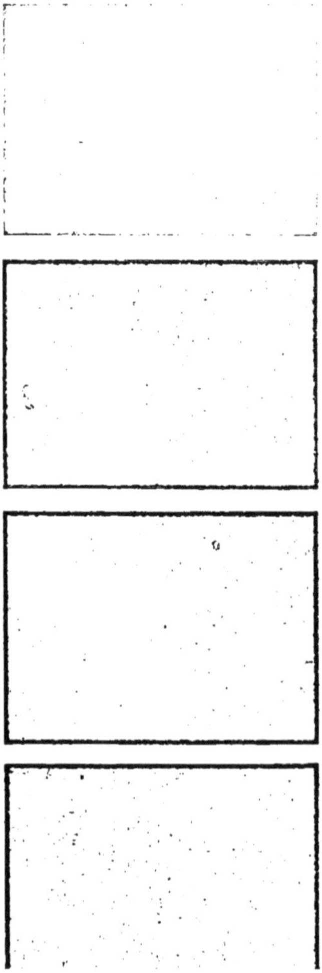

1

2

3

4

Shade	Pattern Number	Parts of Fly dyed to shade
1	25	Body & whisk.
2		
3	2	Horsehair ribbing body.
	32	Body.
4	30	Condor at tail end of body.

PLATE XXII

Yellow Ochre

Page 326 on Colour Chart

Patterns in which materials dyed to the various shades of this colour are used.

Shade	Pattern Number	Parts of Fly dyed to shade
1	6	Body.
2		
3		
4		

PLATE XXIII

Madder Brown

Page 334 on Colour Chart

Patterns in which materials dyed to the various shades of this colour are used.

1 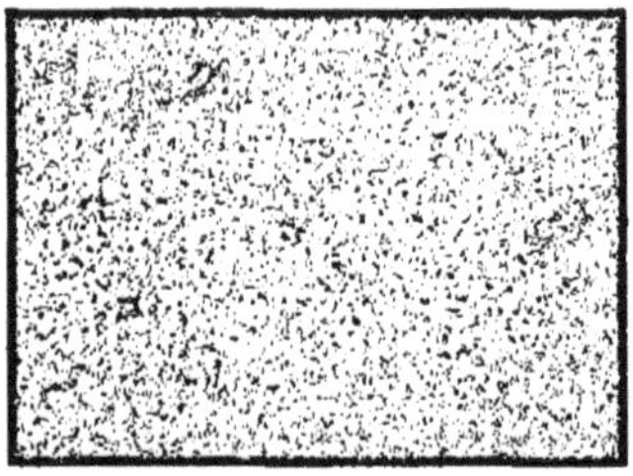

2 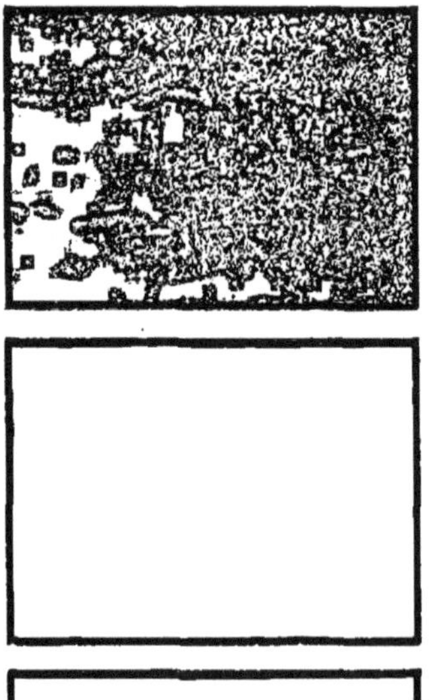

3

4

Shade	Pattern Number	Parts of Fly dyed to shade
1	1	Horsehair ribbing body.
	4	Horsehair ribbing body.
2		
3		
4	24	Condor body.

PLATE XXIV

Van Dyck Brown

Page 340 on Colour Chart

Patterns in which materials dyed to the various shades of this colour are used.

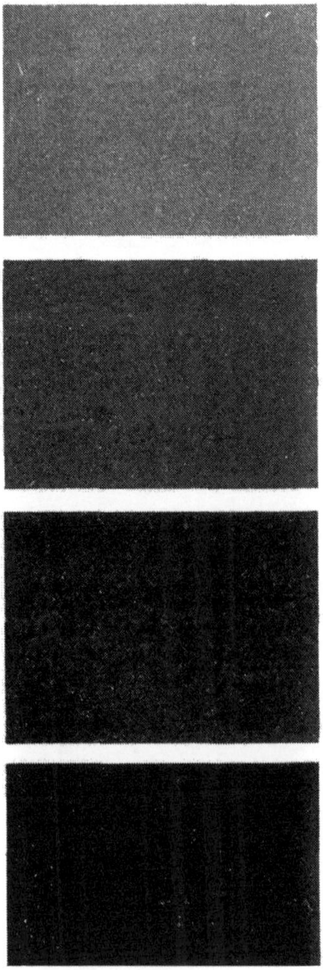

Shade		Pattern Number	Parts of Fly dyed to shade
1	1	24	Horsehair ribbing body.
2	2		
3	3		
4	4	9	Horsehair head.
		11	Horsehair at tail end of body & head.
		18	Horsehair head.
		20	Horsehair at tail end of body

PLATE XXV

Maroon

Page 341 on Colour Chart

Patterns in which materials dyed to the various shades of this colour are used.

Shade	Pattern Number	Parts of Fly dyed to shade
1	7	Horsehair head.
	22	Horsehair head.
	24	Horsehair head.
	26	Horsehair head.
	29	Wings & horsehair ribbing body.
	30	Horsehair ribbing body.
2		
3	21	Body.
	28	Body.
4	11	Horsehair at thorax.
	31	Body.

PLATE XXVI

Dark Chocolate Brown

Page 342 on Colour Chart

Patterns in which materials dyed to the various shades of this colour are used.

Shade	Pattern Number	Parts of Fly dyed to shade
1		
2	16	Horsehair at thorax.
3	29	Body.
	30	Body.
	31	Wings.
4	1	Whisk.
	2	Whisk.
	3	Horsehair ribbing body & whisk.
	4	Whisk.
	5	Horsehair ribbing body & whisk.
	6	Condor ribbing body & whisk.
	20	Horsehair at thorax.

PLATE XXVII

Bluish Black

Page 348 on Colour Chart

Patterns in which materials dyed to the various shades of this colour are used.

1
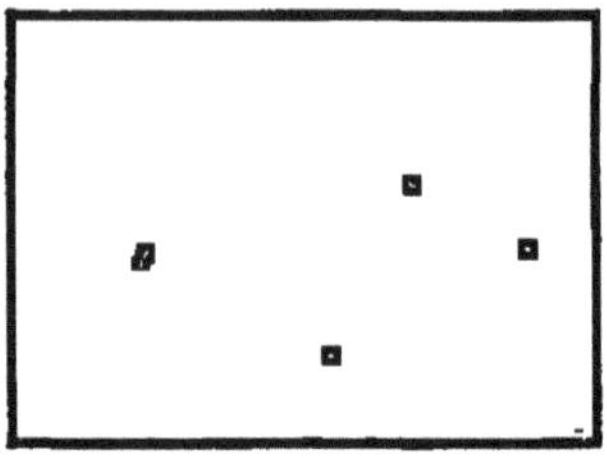

2
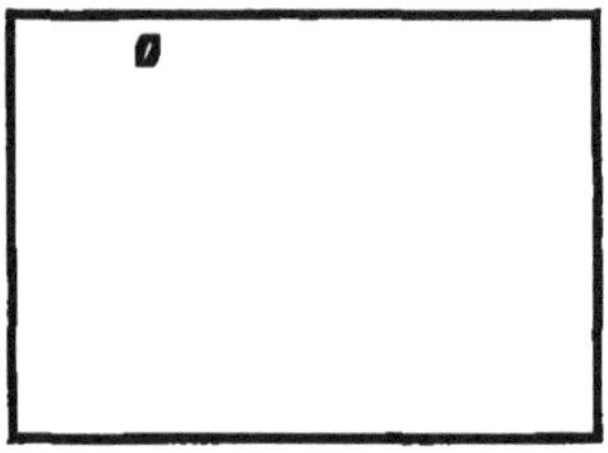

3

4
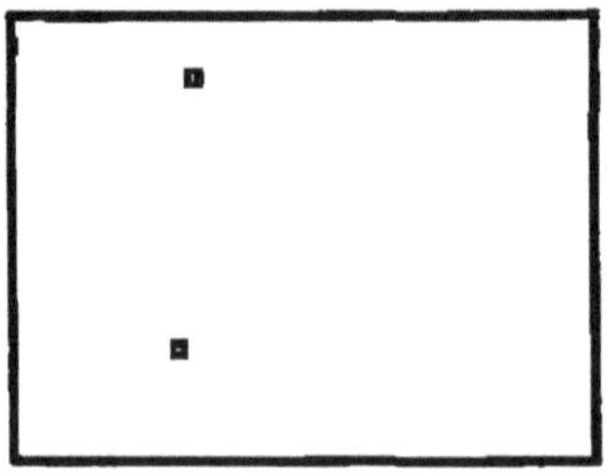

Shade	Pattern Number	Parts of Fly dyed to shade
1	18	Wings.
	19	Wings.
2		
3		
4		

CHAPTER VI

MODERN METHODS OF DRESSING

The tyro is now supposed to have all his tools and materials arranged conveniently in front of him on his working table. The table, when working by daylight, should be placed in a good light facing the window, or after dark the lamp, whether of the electric or candle stamp, should be in front of him in such a position that the light is reflected on to his work, and far enough away to leave room for his fingers holding the tying silk to pass round the hook-shank without coming into contact with the lamp itself. The vice is set up in place with the jaws inclined to the right, the pillar upright, and at a height to suit the convenience of the operator. The hook on which the fly is to be dressed is securely fixed in the jaws of the vice in the position shown in Fig. 4, with the shank in a horizontal position.

It is prudent to test the temper of all hooks before using them. This is done by pulling the eye-end of the shank upwards somewhat sharply. A brittle hook will generally snap off at the bend, and a soft one open out and remain open, while the properly tempered hook will spring back to the horizontal position. Professionals are apt to neglect this very necessary precaution, with the result that the too highly tempered hook will often break off when striking, and the soft one is most likely to open by the strain of playing the fish. In either case it is safe to predict that the fisherman will be disappointed, and the trout or grayling swim away, wiser and more wary from its providential escape.

Break or cut away from the reel about twelve inches of tying silk. The white, cream, and pale yellow are the strongest of the Pearsall gossamer silks, and it is always well to try the strength, because the external part of the silk on the reel very soon gets rotten from exposure to light and air, and nothing is more annoying than to break the silk at a critical moment when dressing the fly. If this should happen, the broken end can be thoroughly waxed as well as a fresh length of tying silk. The new length can be scarfed to the broken end by twisting them up together, or, if the broken end is too short to scarf, the new length should be worked over the old lapping.

Take a piece of wax about the size of a pea and place it in the fold of a small piece of stoutish leather ; this saves the fingers from getting sticky from the wax while waxing the tying silk. Pass the silk round the pillar of the vice and draw the ends tightly together, holding them between the left thumb and forefinger. Open the fold of leather with the wax in it sufficiently to allow it to ride over the silk, held taut in the left thumb and forefinger, and placing the right thumb and forefinger each on one side of the leather, draw it with the wax against the silk backwards and forwards smoothly until the entire length of the tying silk is thoroughly covered with wax. At first one must expect to break the silk very frequently during this operation, but after a time the knack of exerting sufficient pressure to deposit the wax without breaking it is acquired, and once acquired, never forgotten.

Separate the two ends of the waxed silk from between the left thumb and forefinger, so as to use a single thickness of the tying silk. For all flies, small or large, the single thickness is to be preferred as turning out stronger and neater work than the doubled silk, which latter was formerly used in dressing mayflies and other large patterns It will be noted in all the diagrams of fly-dressing given here that the silk is lapped in what some of my readers may deem a left-handed direction. Originally I lapped in the usual direction, but my friend G. S. Marryat persuaded me at an early date in my career as a fly-dresser to adopt his plan. I advise all who can to follow his precedent, because it certainly seems more convenient, and at each lap, when drawing the silk taut, the right hand is below the work, quite clear of it, and the fly in process of dressing is easily seen.

Take one end of the waxed silk between the left thumb and forefinger on the further side of the vice, pass it over the hook just at the neck behind the eye, and holding the silk in the right hand at a distance of about five inches, work three or four turns of it round the hook-shank, laying the folds closely jammed one behind the other, and pulling each fold down as firmly as possible. The expression *behind* in all descriptions of fly-dressing is intended to indicate *towards the bend of the hook or the tail end of the fly*, and the words *in front*, towards *the eye or head of the fly*.

If the silk is thoroughly waxed—and if necessary it should be waxed occasionally during the manipulation—there is no necessity for a weight or any other contrivance to keep the tying silk taut, if it is released, while preparing for the next or any subsequent operation. The fly-tyer should be careful not to let the right thumb and forefinger slip down over the waxed silk while lapping, because this movement must tend to remove some of the wax and make the thumb and finger sticky—both points to be avoided. So far the manipulation is similar for all methods and styles of dressing the patterns.

Dressing an Upright-Winged Dun

For the manipulation of dressing an upright winged dun, the male olive dun No. 7 is selected as a type. It is tied on a No. o hook, and the operator must note that all the diagrams illustrating the *modus operandi* of fly-tying are considerably magnified, so as to show clearly the successive stages of

building up the fly, and the thickness of the tying
silk is shown proportionately very much enlarged,
to indicate distinctly the number of turns or laps
made with it.

The second, third, or fourth primary pinion feather
is detached from each wing of the same starling,
selecting one of medium colour. The central quill
of each is split longitudinally with a sharp penknife,
and the longer plume only retained for use. Remove as much as possible of the pith from the quill,
and cut through the quill into sections of the width
required for a wing, which for a No. o hook is
slightly above $\frac{1}{8}$ inch. Detach two sections from
the right feather, lay one on the other with their
points even, and the darker sides of each downwards.
Treat two sections from the left feather in the same
way. Lay the two sections from the one feather
with the darker sides downwards, and take the two
sections from the other feather with the forceps
and lay them with the points even, the darker
sides upwards, on the first two sections. The four
sections form a pair of wings, and when looked at
edgewise should be in the shape of the letter V,
with the points upwards and diverging.

Lift the pair of wings from the table with the
forceps, take them between the right thumb and
forefinger, and stroke or coax any disarranged fibres
into place. The wings are then transferred to the
left thumb and forefinger, and placed on top of the
hook, just behind the last turn of the tying silk, so

that the natural inclination of the fibres comprising the plume slope to the left or tail end of the fly. The wings are held quite firmly between the thumb and forefinger of the left hand, two or three turns of the tying silk are passed over the wings and round the hook-shank, the left thumb and forefinger being momentarily separated just enough to let the

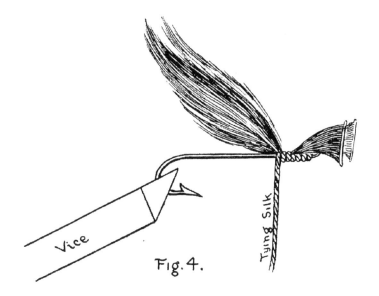

Fig. 4.

silk pass between them. The silk is then drawn quite taut, and kept taut as each turn is firmly and securely pulled down by the right hand. The fly will then appear as shown in Fig. 4.

One turn of the tying silk is then passed behind the wings and over the hook-shank, and pulled tightly forwards. The stability of the work is entirely dependent on the wings being firmly fixed in position. Pull the stumps out horizontally and at right angles to the hook-shank, each pair of stumps on its own side of the hook. The appearance of the fly at this stage is shown in Fig. 5.

Hold the tying silk in the right hand, and simultaneously bring the stumps back behind the wings; take two or three turns behind the wings over the stumps and hook-shank. This action will force the

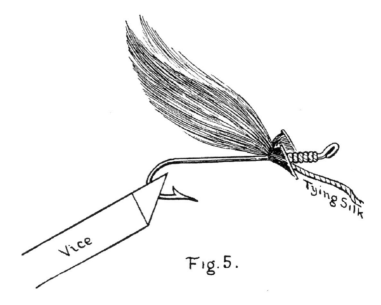

Fig. 5.

wings into an upright position. The wings must be quite plumb and central on the hook-shank when viewed edgewise, and be V-shaped, with the points separated.

Cut away the remainder of the stumps with the scissors, place the two hackles against the hook-shank with their points projecting forwards, and fasten in the stem or root ends of the hackles with three or four firm close turns of the tying silk. The appearance of the fly will then be as shown in Fig. 6.

Continue lapping the hook-shank with the waxed silk until it is within three or four turns of the bend of the hook. Take four strands of Gallina, dyed, of course, to the requisite shade, lay them in position

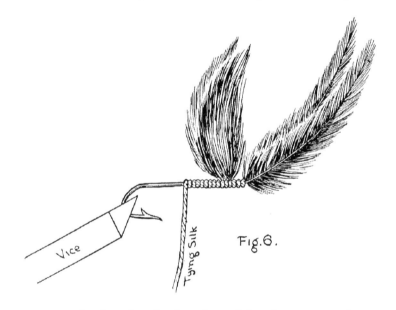

Fig. 6.

on top of the hook-shank with the natural curve of the fibres upwards, and fasten them in with three turns of the tying silk, and take one turn under the whisk and round the hook just at the bend—this tends to set the tail up. Of course, the fly this pattern is intended to imitate has only two setæ, and none of the Ephemeridæ have more than three; but an artificial fly looks better, cocks better, and floats better with as many as four fibres in the whisk.

Lay the strand of quill for the body in position on the hook-shank, the stouter end towards the head of the fly, and the point projecting over the vice; fasten it in with the tying silk, carrying the successive turns evenly up to the shoulder, close behind the wings. Cut off the refuse ends of the quill and whisk. The foundation of the body should

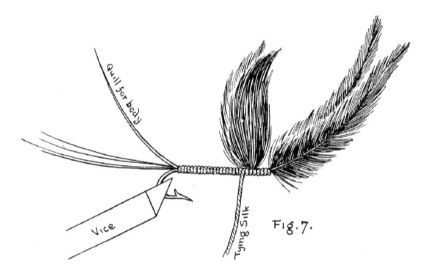

Quill for body
Vice
Tying Silk
Fig. 7.

be smooth and taper slightly, the stouter portion at the shoulder and the finer at the tail end, and it is often necessary to work in a few extra turns of the tying silk, especially towards the shoulder, to effect this. The appearance of the fly is then as shown in Fig. 7.

Work on the quill of the body, laying it in even, smooth folds until it reaches the shoulder, where secure it with two turns of the tying silk and cut away the refuse end of the quill.

When dressing patterns, such as the female olive dun, where the body consists of two quills of different colours, the length of quill for the part at the tail end is tied in as just before described, the tying silk carried up to the point at which the other quill should commence, the tail quill is worked on, secured by the tying silk, and refuse end cut away. The second quill is then placed in position, secured by tying silk, which is carried up to shoulder—the quill is then worked on, secured, and the refuse end cut away.

Fix the point of one hackle in the pliers, place the right forefinger in the ring of the pliers, and keeping the hackle on its edge with the glossy or outer side towards the head of the fly, make a turn of the hackle round the body close behind the wings. With the forefinger in the ring of the pliers, and retaining the hackle in its position, wind it on the hook behind the wings. The position of the forefinger, kept throughout this operation in the ring of the pliers, will counteract the natural tendency of the hackle to twist. When *turning a hackle*—as this operation of winding it on is usually termed—it is always well to bring the pliers well forward when underneath the hook, so as to fill up the space under the wings. When all the hackle has been turned, secure the point with two very firm turns of the waxed silk and cut away the refuse end. Fix the pliers on the second hackle, and the fly will appear as shown in Fig. 8.

Following precisely the same plan, turn the second

hackle, secure the point, cut away the refuse end, and bringing the tying silk in successive folds through the turns of both the hackles to the shoulder. This is a most necessary operation, but unfortunately is too often neglected by the professional fly-dresser, with the result that the fly in use does not last as long as it should. The turns of the hackles should be forced in behind the wings when dressing patterns with upright wings, as this tends to set them up and keep them in the vertical. This forcing the turns of the hackle in behind the wings can also be used to correct the set of the wings in any case if they do not appear to be as upright as those of the natural insect.

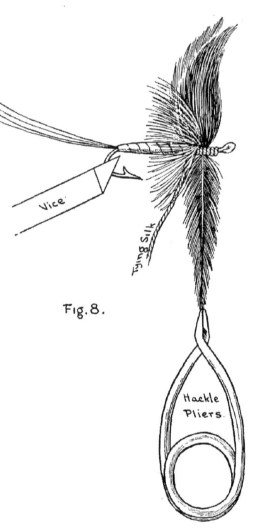

Vice
Tying Silk
Hackle
Pliers.
Fig. 8.

Three turns of horsehair dyed to the requisite

shade are worked on the head of the pattern, the dressing of which is here described, as well as for all the male duns and spinners and the male black gnat. They are placed on the neck of the hook close behind the eye, and are intended to imitate the very prominent turbinate eyes of the males of the genera *Baetis*, *Centroptilum*, and *Ephemerella* among the Ephemeridæ, and also the male of *Bibio johannis*. One end of the horsehair is held in the left hand above the hook-shank on the farther side of the hook, and the other in the right on the nearer side, the three turns are worked round the shank, and both ends held together in the left hand, while a couple of turns of the tying silk are worked over them to secure the horsehair. The refuse end of the horsehair is then cut away closely.

It will be noted that throughout the operation no half-hitch or other knot has been made, and the end of the tying silk has not been fixed by any mechanical means. As before remarked, there is not the smallest necessity for either of these courses, and the old-fashioned plan of making half-hitches at various stages only tended to make the pattern unsightly and served no useful purpose. If the silk is thoroughly waxed at the start and kept waxed during the manipulation, and if after each turn it is firmly pulled down, there should be no tendency on its part to slacken.

All that now remains is to fasten off the fly. There are two ways of doing this, one right and

one wrong. The wrong one is to make a series
of half-hitches, which are neither neat nor secure,
and professionals who use them do not deserve
work from the dry-fly fisherman. The right and
only thoroughly reliable knot for the last operation in tying a floating fly is the *whip finish*. It is
made thus :—Carry the end of the waxed silk back

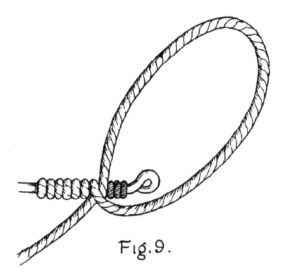

Fig. 9.

towards the tail, leaving an open loop over the
head of the fly. The accompanying Fig. 9 shows
the appearance of the eye end of the hook at this
stage.

Take three or four close turns of the loop over
the shank and the end of the tying silk close behind
but clear of the turns of horsehair at the head.
Fig. 10 shows the appearance of the eye and of
the hook at this stage.

Holding the right thumb and forefinger over

the turns of silk so as to soften the wax slightly by the warmth of the fingers, draw with the left hand the end of the tying silk firmly and *slowly* until it is quite tight and smooth. A little patience

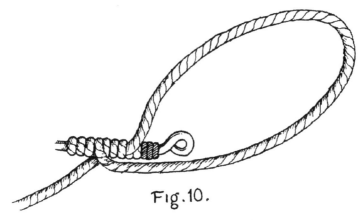

Fig. 10.

will generally accomplish this, and any impatience will probably result in a fracture of the silk and the necessity for working on a new length of tying silk and making the head look clumsy. Fig. 11 shows the end of the hook at this stage.

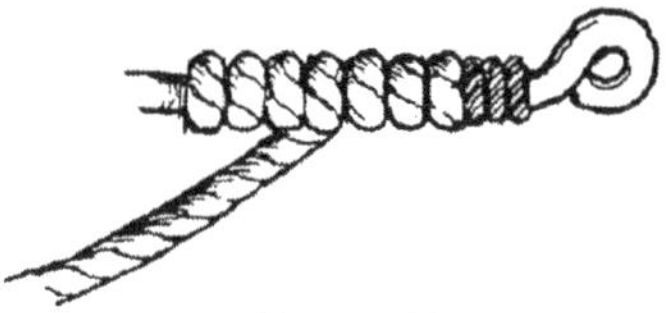

Fig. 11.

Break or cut off the loose end of the tying silk, and roll the fingers over the knot to make it quite smooth. Touch the head with varnish, and the fly is complete. If a few fibres of the hackle are out of place, they can generally be coaxed back into position by laying the fly flat on the table and brushing it over with a short and very stiff tooth-brush, which should be kept for the purpose.

When dressing flat-winged flies the wings are set on and tied in as before described, but the stumps, instead of being pulled out horizontally at right angles to the hook-shank, are cut off closely, and two very tight turns of the tying silk laid over the stumps.

If the pattern is one without ribbing hackle, such as the welshman's button, black gnat female,

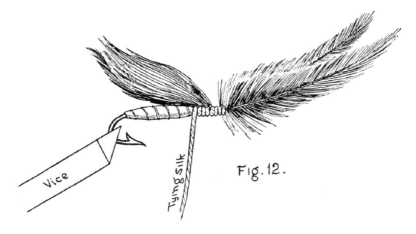

Fig. 12.

or brown ant, two hackles are tied in as described for the upright-winged dun, and the tying silk carried down in successive turns to the bend of the hook. The body materials and horsehair or other ribbing used in the pattern are laid in position, tied in with a few turns of silk, the refuse cut off, and the tying silk carried up to the shoulder. The body is then formed and secured and refuse cut off, and the ribbing also worked on in open turns, secured, and refuse cut off. The fly then has the appearance as seen in Fig. 12.

First one shoulder hackle and then the second one is turned, but the turns are not jammed in behind the wings, as it is not desired to force them up into a vertical position, and the first two or three turns of the second hackle are carried round the hook-shank in front of the wings. This is an important point, and it may be here noted that the set of wings can always be corrected to a certain extent by remembering that the greater the number of turns of hackle behind the wings, the more they are forced towards a vertical position ; and the greater the number of turns in front of the wings, the flatter the wings will lie. The wings of a flat-winged pattern should incline approximately at an angle of 30° to the hook-shank. One of the most prevalent faults of the modern professional fly-dressers is a tendency to dress patterns like black gnats, sedges, ants, &c., with wings in the upright position required for the duns.

If the pattern to be dressed has a ribbing hackle, the flat wings are set on as before described, and three hackles are tied in, two shoulder hackles and one ribbing hackle. When selecting these it should be noted that the ribbing hackle must be a trifle shorter in the fibre than the shoulder hackles. The tying silk is carried down to the bend of the hook, and the body material as well as a short length of waxed silk are tied in, and the tying silk carried up to the shoulder. The short length of waxed silk tied in at the tail end of the fly should be as nearly as possible of the same colour as the body material.

The ribbing hackle is fixed in the hackle pliers and turned in open folds down to the bend of the hook, when the fly will appear as shown in Fig. 13. The point of the ribbing hackle is secured by two or three turns of the waxed silk at the tail end of the fly,

Waxed Silk
Vice
Hackle
Pliers
Tying Silk

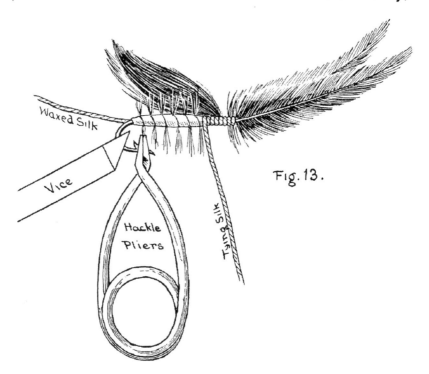

Fig. 13.

and the waxed silk is then wound in open turns over the ribbing hackle to the shoulder. If the fibres of the hackle are set approximately at right angles to the hook-shank and the waxed silk is lapped in the same direction as the ribbing hackle, it can be easily coaxed clear of the fibres of the hackles and secure each turn of it. The end of the waxed silk which has just been worked up from the tail end of

the fly is then secured by the tying silk and the refuse
end cut off.

First one shoulder hackle and then the other is
turned, but, as before remarked, the turns are not
jammed in behind the wings, as it is not desired to
set them upright. After the second hackle has been
secured, the flat-winged fly, whether with or without
ribbing hackle, is finished with the whip finish and a
touch of varnish.

Dressing Spinners with Hackle-point Wings

The type of fly taken to describe this method is
No. 11, the male olive spinner, dressed with two
medium blue dun cock hackles for wings, a putty-
coloured shoulder hackle, body and thorax in three
colours of horsehair, a whisk of putty colour, and
three turns of dark Van Dyck brown horsehair at
the head.

After the first turns of waxed silk have been
worked round the neck of the hook, take the two
hackles and strip the down and fibres from the root
end of them until the points are the correct length for
the wings, remembering that they must be a trifle
shorter than the length of the hook-shank. Place
these two hackles on the table with the glossy sides
upwards, one on the other, so that the last fibres of
each are in juxtaposition, and place them on top of
the hook immediately behind the last turn of tying
silk on the neck of the hook. The accompanying

diagram, Fig. 14, shows the appearance of the fly at this stage in plan.

Secure the hackle-point wings by two or three very firm turns of the tying silk, worked diagonally in both directions, taking great care to keep the wings quite flat on the top of the hook. Press

Hackle
Vice
Hackle
Tying Silk

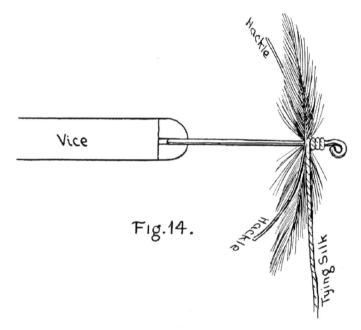

Fig. 14.

the stump ends of the two hackles back, secure them behind the wings, and cut off the refuse ends as closely as possible. The hackle is then fixed in position with its point over the head of the fly. One hackle is sufficient for all the hackle-point winged spinners, but if the fisherman is afraid of a little extra labour in drying the fly he can use two hackles, although in this case the pattern will certainly appear bulky and heavy as compared with the natural insect.

Until the plan of making the bodies as described herein was devised, the patterns of the male spinners of the olive, iron-blue, and pale watery duns had an unnatural opaque appearance in the bodies, and were not much appreciated by the highly educated trout of the Hampshire trout streams. The underlying principle of the modern method of building up the horsehair bodies is that there should be no tying silk

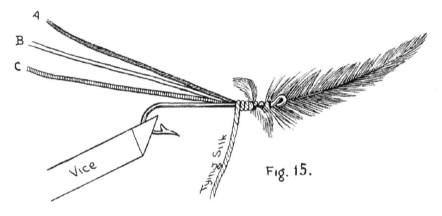

Fig. 15.

or other opaque substance between the semi-transparent horsehair and the hook-shank. Of course the hook itself is opaque, but the spinner dressed after this fashion has a very light and translucent appearance.

The three horsehairs required to form the body are fastened in at the shoulder by the tying silk, and on the diagram, Fig. 15, the fly is shown at this stage—A being the dark maroon horsehair representing the thorax of the natural insect, B the dull yellow-green horsehair, the central part of the body, and C the dark Van Dyck brown horsehair at the tail end of the body.

Take the horsehair A and make four close turns round the hook-shank over the horsehairs B and C, which will lie flat along the top of the hook. Fix the end of A in the hackle pliers and leave it hanging. In a previous part of this chapter it has been said that there is no occasion to fix the tying silk at any time during the successive operations of fly-dressing, and for fear the reader should think that I am recanting this opinion I reiterate it here. The horsehair, however, is of quite a different nature, and there is no wax on it to assist in making it adhere to the hook, so that it is essential in making these bodies to suspend the hackle pliers in order to keep the horsehair from slackening while proceeding to the next operation.

Take the horsehair B and make eleven close turns round the hook with it over the horsehair C, which should lie flat along the top of the hook-shank, and leave the end of B hanging with another pair of hackle pliers holding it.

Lay the four fibres of gallina for the whisk in position along the top of the hook, and with the natural inclination of the feather concave and turned upwards. Secure the whisk with three turns of the horsehair C, which should finish at the bend of the hook. Leave the end of C hanging down in the jaws of a third pair of hackle pliers, and cut the refuse ends of the fibres forming the whisk as closely as possible. Working back towards the head of the fly, take three close turns of C over the three turns taken before, and leave the end hanging in the pliers. Fig. 16 will give the appearance of the fly at this stage, except that the three pairs of hackle pliers have been purposely omitted, to show clearly the positions of the three horsehairs.

Draw the end of the horsehair C forwards, and holding it down firmly with the right hand, take

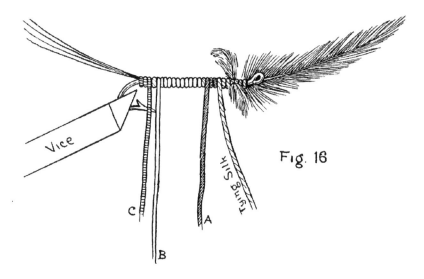

Fig. 16

the horsehair B in the left and make a very firm turn of it round the hook and over C to secure it. Remove the pliers from C and cut off the refuse end closely. Take eleven turns of B, which, with the single already made to secure C, will complete the number of twelve as specified in the description of the dressing. Bring the end of B forward, secure it with a turn of A, and cut away the refuse end of B. Take three turns of the horsehair, which, with the single one made to secure B, will make up the specified number of four. Secure the end of A with the tying silk and cut off the refuse end of A, and the fly will look like the diagram, Fig. 17.

The reader will note that the turns of horsehair forming the body are now composed throughout of two thicknesses worked one over the other. The number of turns of horsehair specified are the requisite number for a No. o hook of correct length of shank, and the number will have to be decreased

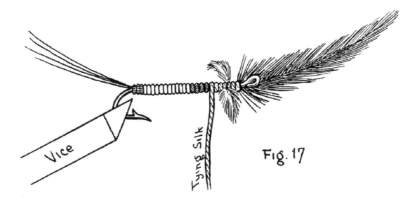

Fig. 17

in the case of spinners, such as the male pale watery and male iron blue, dressed on No. oo hooks. The process of making these horsehair bodies may appear complicated, but when the operator has once mastered them he will realise that there is no real difficulty in carrying them out, especially if he uses the horsehair from the violin bow, as recommended before.

Turn the hackle in the ordinary way, secure it with the tying silk, carry the tying silk through the turns of the hackle to the shoulder. Work the horsehair for the head as described for the male olive dun, complete the fly with the whip finish and the touch of varnish.

When dressing hackle-point winged spinners like the females of the olive, pale watery, and iron blue, and both sexes of the sherry spinner, after winging, the remaining operations follow almost precisely that of dressing the upright-winged dun. The stem end of the hackle (one hackle only) is fastened in, the tying silk is carried to the bend of the hook, the whisk secured in place, the body material (with or without ribbing horsehair, according to the pattern) is fastened in, the tying silk carried to shoulder, the body formed and secured, the tackle turned and secured, and the fly finished as usual.

To Dress a Mayfly

After the tying silk has been worked on the neck of the hook, a pair of feathers from the breast or back of a Rouen drake or mallard of suitable length and shape are taken in the left thumb and forefinger and the down stripped from the root ends of the stems. The length of the wings having been carefully judged, the remainder of the plumes are worked down with the right thumb and forefinger moistened. The wings are applied to the hook, each stem, with the plume on it, on the proper side of the hook, and securely fastened by three or four turns of the tying silk. The appearance of the fly is then as shown in Fig. 18.

Press the stems of the wings back, and take one turn of the tying silk over them behind the wings. Carry the tying silk between and round the wings close down to and above the hook-shank in a figure of eight, and take two or three turns of the tying silk tightly round the bases of both wings horizontally. The object of the figure of eight and horizontal lapping round the stems is to strengthen the central

Vice
Tying Silk
Stems of Wings

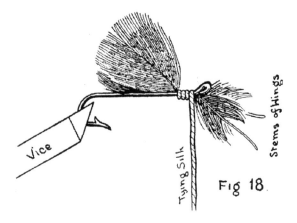

Fig 18.

quill of the wings close down to the hook, and neglect of this precaution is one of the reasons why the professional's mayflies do not stand, and why the wings so often turn round in use. If one or both of the wings come away altogether while fishing, it may safely be conjectured that the fly-dresser has neglected to turn the stems of the pattern back—a piece of laziness and neglect which is almost unpardonable. The close-plumed feather prepared as previously described is fastened in, and then the two shoulder hackles, the fly appearing as shown in Fig. 19.

Many critics have found fault with the modern plan of representing the six legs of a natural insect by three hackles, and some have enunciated the theory that coming short to the mayfly is due to this profligate superfluity of legs. They may be right, although personally I am not in accord with them, my experience being that a fish feeding on mayfly seldom

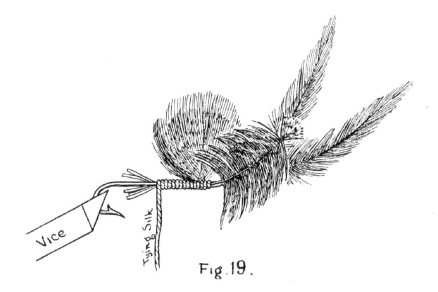

Fig. 19.

comes short to a floating imitation of it, and that as a general rule the trout that does not fasten to the artificial fly is one feeding on the nymphs or on some other insect, probably the welshman's button or the pupa of this fly as it is coming to the surface to effect its metamorphosis to the winged stage. They must remember, too, that this profusion of legs is almost necessary to assist in floating the large hook on which the fly is dressed.

The remaining manipulation of dressing the mayfly is carried out as usual, except of course that there are three hackles to turn instead of two.

DRESSING THE SPENT GNATS

Take four Andalusian cock hackles (dark for the male and medium for the female), selecting the best shaped and marked ones procurable. They should be glossy and have a suspicion of warm honey or ginger marking in the points of the fibres. Strip from the stem ends all the down and fibres so as to leave only sufficient of the points to form the wings. Here again remember that the length of the wings is slightly less than the length of the body and thorax of the natural insect.

Lay the two hackles for the wing on the further side of the hook, evenly one on the other, with the glossy sides upwards and the stems turning towards you. Then lay the two hackles for the wing on the side of the hook nearer to you, similarly with the glossy sides upwards and the stems directed away from you. Place the two hackles forming the wing on the further side on the two hackles forming the wing on the nearer side so that the last fibres left on the hackles coincide, and place the four hackles forming the pair of wings quite flat on the bare hook-shank immediately behind the three or four turns of tying silk already worked on the neck of the hook. They will then appear as shown in plan in Fig. 20.

Work the tying silk diagonally in both directions over the stems of the hackles and the hook-shank, taking the greatest care to keep the wings quite flat, and making them as secure as possible by pulling down each turn of the tying silk as taut as possible without the risk of breaking the silk. The appear-

Hackle
Hackle
Vice
Hackle
Tying Silk
Hackle

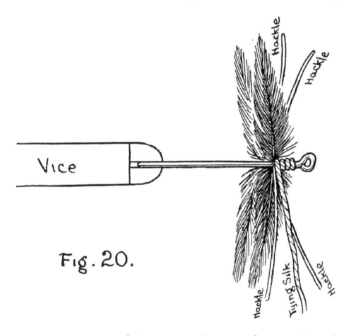

Fig. 20.

ance of the fly at this stage is as shown in plan in the diagram, Fig. 21.

The stems of the four hackles are then forced back against the hook-shank and secured with a couple of turns close behind the wings. When dressing the female spent gnat the two shoulder hackles are then laid in position and secured, and the fly will look like the diagram in plan, Fig. 22.

When dressing the male the close-plumed dark

grouse head hackle properly prepared, as before described, is placed in position first, and then the two

Hackle
Hackle
Vice
Tying Silk
Hackle
Hackle

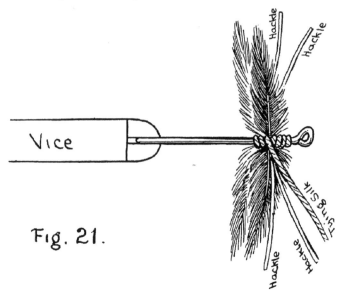

Fig. 21.

shoulder hackles. The tying silk is carried down to the bend of the hook, the four strands of gallina being

Vice
Tying Silk

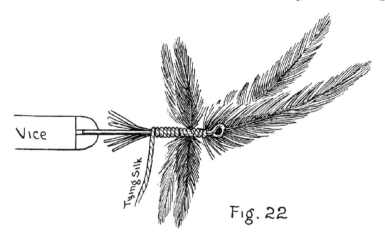

Fig. 22

fixed in position for the whisk, and a single turn of the tying silk made immediately behind and under the whisk and over the hook-shank. The body material and ribbing are then fastened in, the tying silk carried to the shoulder, the body and ribbing formed and secured, the hackles turned and secured, not omitting the carrying of the tying silk through the turns of the hackle to the neck, where the fly is finished by the whip finish and a touch of varnish is applied.

Methods of fly-dressing are always to some extent matters of opinion, and experienced operators who have adopted a different order of procedure may perhaps not be inclined to depart from their usual plan. If their results please them I should be the last to urge them to change in any way, and I have the greatest respect for the notions and ideas of those who differ from me. The point on which probably the methods described herein will be subjected to the most damaging criticism is the advice to put on the wings of all patterns as the first operation.

Such of my readers as are *cocksure*, whether from sufficiently or insufficiently sound and considered reasons, will, I fear, not allow themselves to be influenced by any argument I could adduce from my own experience. I would, however, confidently appeal to any who are in doubt to give the plan of fixing the wings in position and securing them as the first process of dressing winged flies on eyed hooks a fair and prolonged trial before condemning it. I venture to predict that a great majority will find that it is the best plan and therefore adopt it for their own work.

PART II

CHAPTER I

CRITICISM OF THE PATTERNS

THE first part of this book is a serious attempt to treat exhaustively of the origin of the new patterns, the selection of the natural insects to be taken as specimens, the matching of the colours, the details of the dressings of the flies, the tools and materials required to make them, with a full chapter on the modern and improved methods of manipulation in tying the flies.

The advantage of being able to carry thirty-three patterns in all, instead of a hundred or more, must appeal to every dry-fly fisherman. He cannot, however, be expected to pin his faith on the new and discard the old standards until it has been conclusively proved to his satisfaction that, so far from this course tending to diminish his bag, it is likely to result in a decided improvement both in his sport and in his comfort.

This is the object to which this second part of the book is devoted, and it contains a number of examples from the author's practical experience of cases where he deems it fairly demonstrated that the use of the new patterns has enabled him to score under conditions when with the old patterns his success would have been problematical at the least.

There are two difficulties to be overcome before the theory can be considered as established.

Firstly, the fact that on certain days and under certain conditions the fish, apparently or actually feeding on the natural insects which the patterns are dressed to imitate, cannot be tempted to rise to the artificial fly. It has always been so, and various reasons have been adduced to account for the vagaries of the trout and grayling on such days. To dismiss the subject airily by postulating the statement that it is due to some atmospheric, climatic, electrical, or other natural cause, sounds very plausible. Perhaps it is sounder and fairer to admit that, with our limited knowledge of the habits, tastes, and general proclivities of the fish, we are unable to find a valid reason for their seemingly eccentric behaviour.

Secondly, we have the fact that there is here and there an experienced dry-fly man so entirely wedded to his old notions, and so essentially in his nature *laudator temporis acti*, that no argument, no array of facts, no consensus of opinion on the other side can induce him to yield one iota of his faith in the artificial flies as used in the days of Walton and Cotton or described by Ronalds more than seventy years ago. We must all respect his opinions, admire his constancy, but deplore the state of mind of one who cannot allow of progress, and even science, effecting a revolution and improving the artificial flies by making them better imitations of the natural insects they are intended to represent in colour, form, and size.

One of the results of attempting to produce a new set of patterns is that a number of friends have entered into correspondence with me about them. Some have approved of them very highly and decided to adopt them. Some have utterly condemned them, but the majority have suspended their judgment until they have had further experience of their use. I find, however, that very few have followed my example of using no other patterns for a course of years. One of my oldest angling friends, bearing a name which must under all circumstances appeal to the lover of the dry fly—Mr. H. S. Hall—has dealt with the question in so logical and temperate a manner that I propose quoting part of his letter and discussing the points raised, from every point of view, whether adverse or the opposite.

I will proceed to an analysis of some of the most salient features in Mr. Hall's letter. In one sentence he says: " I must confess that, except with regard to the spinners, I do not see anything very different from what I have used already;" and later he remarks: " The spinners present varieties which are new to me, and which I shall have some interest in trying when next I have a chance of fishing" The reference here is to the duns and their spinners, and not to the mayflies, which are not very plentiful on the Wiley, the stream he fishes.

He is quite right, as beyond an attempt, which I think has been fairly successful, to improve the colouration of the smaller Ephemeridæ in the sub-imago state, they do not in any marked degree vary from patterns previously dressed. Surely, however, to produce imitations which not only in colour but in form and size are far more like the natural insects than the old standard flies, is a very decided step in advance. The spinners or imagines are in quite a different category, and, as already shown in a previous chapter, were the outcome of Mr. Williamson's persistence in impressing upon me the necessity of devising better imitations of these than had previously been dressed. This idea of tying all spinners with flat hackle-point wings was the mainspring of the movement that has culminated in the present patterns, which I would humbly suggest are the very best imitations of the natural insects extant.

To quote further from Mr. Hall's letter :—

" The olives vary a great deal in shades at different times, and it puzzles me how any one can produce a shade which is *the* shade for any particular fly. Last year in October I found the Wiltshire grayling very particular indeed. No olives which

I had (and I had four or five different shades)
seemed to be right. After catching several natural
flies I came to my own conclusion as to what was
wanted, and sent off four patterns from my stock,
giving instructions that the body was to be of
A shade, wings of B shade, legs of C shade, size
D, and the result was a fly which the fish took
better than any I had before used. But my fly is
not represented by either of the patterns, dark or
light."

My friend may be right in saying that the
colouration of the olives on the Wiltshire streams
varies "a great deal at different times," but this
does not accord with my own experience of the
Test and Itchen. When collecting specimens for
matching, I take *from the water only* a large number
of the same species. I find that the great majority
of the same sex are approximately the same shade
and the same size, with a few occasional, and I would
urge *abnormal*, specimens varying in colour or size.
The males and females are quite distinct both in
colour and size, the male generally darker and
smaller than the female. There are two distinct
colourations of true olives, the common olive (which
in the series is called the *olive*) and the dark olive,
so that with the two sexes there are obviously four
colours of olive. My friend's instructions to make
the "body of A shade, wings of B shade, legs of
C shade, size D," follow so closely on the lines of
the matching done by me that I am not surprised

to hear that "the result was a fly which the fish took far better than any I had before used."

Mr. Hall asked later in the same letter: "When olives are coming down, are there not both males and females coming down together? Do the fish discriminate between them so that they refuse all of one sex and feed only on the other? If not, I cannot see the necessity of imitating both sexes."

Entomologists have observed that certainly with the Ephemeridæ, and probably with many other families of insects, the earliest individuals to assume the winged state are almost exclusively the males, and as a rule the males greatly outnumber the females. Thus at times the olives coming down are mostly males, and at a later period the majority are females, and it is quite conceivable that an imitation would prove more tempting to a fish rising if it represented the sex which was predominant in the water at the moment.

Criticism like Mr. Hall's, which is based on opinions formed after due consideration and on reasoned and reasonable grounds, cannot be objected to by any one who is prepared to listen to the other side of the question, but the class of adverse criticism generally encountered is not at all of this description. Anglers often tell me that they like the new patterns and have adopted them, but that one of the old standards, say the red quill, has been so successful that they invariably add this to the collection and carry a thirty-fourth pattern.

The red quill is in all probability taken as an imitation and, I would urge, an inferior imitation, of the same insect that the female olive (red) spinner or spent imago of the female olive is intended to represent. It does not seem likely that it should be successful when the new pattern, which is truer to nature, has been tried and has failed. I can quite imagine that one who has a *penchant* for a particular fancy pattern will insist on using it at times, and I can forgive him, for, after all, as before said, "nothing tends so much to success in a particular pattern of fly as an ineradicable conviction in the mind of the fisherman that it is infallible."

It must be admitted, however, that so far there has been little if any hostile demonstration against the new patterns, and a number of the most experienced chalk-stream fishermen use them in preference to any others. Many of the professional dressers are to blame for the careless way in which they have matched their colours, and in some instances the size of the pattern has not been adhered to. For the future there can be no excuse for this, seeing that the colours of all the dyed materials can be matched with the colour chart, and the dressings, which include the size of the hook, are now described in detail.

My own experience of the exclusive use of the new patterns during the 1904 season was so satisfactory that I am tempted to recapitulate it in tabulated form. Two days on the Test contributed eight trout, but the remainder all came from the Itchen, and about 80 per cent of these from the St. Cross water. Few of the fish returned were very small, a large proportion being liberated on the well-known and admirable principle of giving them the benefit of the doubt when they were just about sizable. Out of the total of 306 trout, 146 were taken with duns, 111 with spinners, and 2 with mayfly, or no less than 259 in all with imitations of the Ephemeridæ. Sedges were responsible for 17, and welshman's button for 10, or 27 in all with Trichoptera, the balance being made up by 9 with male black gnats and 11 with brown ants. The small number falling victims to the mayfly was due to my not being on the spot when the fish took it, and the sedges would certainly have scored more heavily but for the fact that I seldom, if ever, fish when the evening light renders it difficult to distinguish the fly on the water.

The following is the table referred to .—

Name of Pattern	Number of Trout killed or returned
Brown mayfly (male)	2
Olive dun (male)	39
Olive dun (female)	39
Dark olive dun (male)	2
Dark olive dun (female)	7
	—
Carry forward	89

Name of Pattern	Number of Trout killed or returned
Brought forward	89
Pale watery dun (male)	13
Pale watery dun (female)	26
Iron-blue (male)	13
Iron-blue (female)	6
Blue-winged olive (male)	1
Olive spinner (female)	24
Olive (red) spinner (female)	44
Pale watery spinner (female)	11
Iron-blue spinner (female)	11
Sherry spinner (male)	8
Sherry spinner (female)	13
Black gnat (male)	9
Brown ant	11
Welshman's button (male)	10
Small dark sedge	16
Medium sedge	1
TOTAL	306

The next year, 1905, I migrated to the Test,
fishing a comparatively short length of water, on
which the work of killing down coarse fish and re-
plenishing the stock of trout had only been carried
on for two years. When the work was commenced
this fishery was at the lowest possible ebb, containing
a large number of pike, many of large size, and as a
natural consequence the trout in it were very few and
generally of large dimensions. Under these conditions
it is not surprising to find that the number of trout
taken was very much less than the bag of 1904.
Thirty-five trout in all were killed on this length

of water during the season, and are tabulated as follows :—

	Number of Trout killed
Spent gnat (male)	5
Olive dun (male)	1
Olive dun (female)	5
Dark olive dun (male)	2
Dark olive dun (female)	1
Olive spinner (female)	1
Olive (red) spinner (female)	2
Iron-blue dun (male)	1
Iron-blue dun (female)	1
Blue-winged olive (female)	1
Brown ant	1
Welshman's button (male)	6
Small dark sedge	5
Medium sedge	1
Cinnamon sedge	2
TOTAL	35

The total is too small to enable any one to arrive at anything like a well-considered opinion as to the relative efficacy of the various patterns. The season was a bad one all round, and the stretch of the Test was still in the transition stage, suffering partly from the neglect of ages and partly from the fact that the new stock introduced had not had the chance of arriving at a size in proportion to the limit voluntarily imposed, viz. 2 lbs. for females and $1\frac{1}{2}$ lbs. for males. I am quite sure, however, that the new patterns did comparatively better than the old ones. I do not compare the records of the other rods on the same length, because one—a first-rate performer—had fished very little, and the other was a comparative tyro in the use of the dry fly.

In 1906 I took over the length of the Test referred to, and since that date have controlled it and fished it with my personal friends only. The stocking and general management, with the assistance of a very capable and intelligent keeper, have been carried on in what may fairly be described as a somewhat extravagantly liberal scale, and the sport has been almost up to our expectations No patterns except the new ones have been used by me, and even where my friends were concerned it is quite the exception to record in the diary the killing of fish with flies other than those comprised in the new series of patterns.

CHAPTER II

MAYFLIES AND SPENT GNATS

THE old-fashioned hatch of mayflies, which has been
described in such high-flown language by many of
the old school of authorities on the subject, seems to
have " gone away mit de lagerbier, avay in die ewig-
keit." For many years the quantity seen on the
Hampshire chalk streams has been an ever-decreas-
ing one. Some of us confidently predict that it will
within a measurable space of time be a rarity, if not
positively non-existent, and that our grandchildren
will not credit the stories told of the numbers seen
in bygone days.

Even on the Kennet, a river which from time immemorial has been held forth as *par excellence* the
mayfly stream of the south, it is scarcely worth while
fishing it on the uppermost reaches, and on some of
the middle and lower stretches it does not show
up in anything like the cloud one used to see in
olden times during the early days of June. Many
anglers will be interested to hear of an opinion expressed by competent observers that there are now
distinct signs of recovery after several bad years.

The first year of our tenancy of the Ramsbury
water was 1893, when the rise of mayfly was a sight

to be remembered. The roads and the meadows in the vicinity of the Kennet were full of the dead and dying insects ; each blade of grass, each bough, was crowded with the subimagines waiting for their metamorphosis to the imago stage, and the air was literally black with the swarms of the male imagines dancing up and down ; and this state of affairs continued for a full three weeks.

There is a good anecdote told *à propos* of an angler who, without previous experience of the river, rented a Kennet fishery, and some days before the expected advent of the mayfly was on the spot, "eager for the fray." Wiling away his time by yarning with the keeper, who was a native of these parts, he asked him in a chaffing tone about the appearance of the country during one of these great hatches. He said : "I suppose that a fisherman requires to wear a respirator to keep them out of his mouth when walking by the side of the river."

"Lor' bless you, sir," said the keeper, "them there respirators ain't a mossel of good. In a proper season we has to get out the snow-plough to clear 'em off the roads." Possibly this may be a little highly coloured, but I can well remember that when the end of the drake season had come, walking along the roads in the gloaming, one was literally crushing the spent gnats under foot at every step, with a distinct *pop* as their hollow bodies collapsed under one's weight.

Dry-fly men are divided roughly into two schools

One consists of the lovers of the mayfly, who deplore the loss of the few days' mad excitement when, during the height of the drake season, they could slaughter great numbers of trout, well above the average size of the denizens of the particular river they fished Some of them are to be included in the category of those whose great ambition of life in any department of sport is to beat their own or other people's records.

There is a second set of men who, so far from regretting the loss or diminution in numbers of the mayfly, welcome it as tending to improve their sport, urging with persistence that the trout take the smaller Ephemeridæ, whether in the subimago or imago stages, better now than they did in the olden times when the mayfly was more plentiful. There is, too, in this set an extreme school of purists who stigmatise mayfly fishing as a form of legalised poaching, somewhat akin to the worm or the minnow.

My own view is that the sport of killing fish approaching or exceeding the 2 lb average, with duns and spinners on 0 or 00 hooks, should be classed as far above that of getting the same or a larger number on mayflies and spent gnats dressed on No. 2 or No 3 or even larger hooks. There is certainly one respect in which the presence of mayflies in sufficient numbers to bring the big fish on the rise is a distinct benefit to the river. This is that the abnormally large male fish, which are almost as destructive to the naturally bred yearling trout as pike, are generally killed in considerable numbers during a favourable mayfly season.

The keeper who understands his business and has his employer's interests at heart can do a great deal to keep down such fish. In the spawning season he can and should get out, by all and every means in his power—fair or foul—as many of these long, lanky, lean, and hungry cannibals as he can, and knock them on the head. Personally I have been fortunate in finding a keeper who, to my mind, is a pattern of what such a man should be, and I mention this here because I should like to place on record my full appreciation of the success which has rewarded his unremitting exertions in carrying out his and my own ideas for improving the sport of the fishery.

It is a source of deep regret to me that since the new patterns were brought out there has not been a single season in which the drake fishing can have been deemed satisfactory. Perhaps the number of fish killed by me with these patterns, although comparatively few in the aggregate, constitute in some respects a more crucial test of their excellence than the slaying of far greater numbers when every trout in the water is rising madly at the natural insect and taking any artificial bearing the smallest resemblance to it

The earliest mayflies seen by me on the lower stretches of the Itchen in 1903 (the first year in which I began to use the new patterns systematically)

were observed on the 23rd May, and even at this date one of those secured was a female imago just ovipositing. We all anticipated from this an early and successful drake season, but on the part of the St. Cross water where the various species of *Ephemera* are plentiful there was no rise until the 1st June. It was a fine warm day, with fresh north-east wind, and during the afternoon, fishing with the green mayfly male, Williamson killed three good trout and a grayling of 2 lbs 6 oz. One of his friends landed a male trout of 2 lbs. 9 oz. in fairly good condition, and a second nearly $1\frac{1}{2}$ lbs., while I secured three trout aggregating $3\frac{3}{4}$ lbs. On the next day, in very similar weather, with the same pattern I succeeded in killing a single trout of 1 lb. 2 oz.

On the 8th June, this, one of the poorest rises of mayfly I can remember on the Itchen, was over for the season, and a visit to a friend's water the next day convinced me that the mayfly season on the Test was also practically over by this date. I am, however, very desirous of calling the reader's attention to an episode which occurred on that day, and which should be deemed a strong proof of the efficacy of the pattern.

The Test in this part is divided into two branches. The larger or eastern branch for nearly half a mile is a deadish deep reach, which in those days contained a few large trout, and it is to be feared a considerable number of pike and other coarse fish. The smaller or western branch is at a lower level, and at a point in my friend's fishery the water of the large stream is penned up to drive what was then a flour-mill, the tail water of which is discharged into and swells the volume of the small stream to such an extent that below this it becomes the larger river and is, in fact, the main stream.

The level of the water above the mill is controlled by a large set of hatches, and the waste water is carried down to a rough shallow forming a continuation of the eastern branch of the river. A carriage road passes over the waste hatches, and there are always a number of large fish rising, especially during the mayfly season, where the stream commences to bifurcate, one part flowing towards the mill and the other to the waste hatches.

After many years' study of the place, my late friend Marryat and I came to the conclusion that the only place from which these fish could be cast to with any chance of success was the road, and the distance being something like twenty-five yards, it was not an easy matter to place the fly accurately and delicately over the feeding trout. The smallest inaccuracy would either make the artificial drag, or in some cases make it float down one stream when the fish was rising on the other. It must be quite understood that in speaking of the bifurcation of the stream I do not intend to convey to the reader the notion that the two forks flow each between its own banks, but that the stream divides in the middle of a broad piece of water, and between these two streams there is a wedge of comparatively still or slow-running water.

The day in question was hazy and chilly in the early morning, with light north-easterly wind, gradually veering to the south-east, and the afternoon was dull, hot, and sunless Wandering about all over the water, I failed to see the rise of a sizable fish before lunch, and the iron-blues, which were hatching out in considerable numbers, were quite neglected by the fish. During lunch my friend told me that it had been a very poor season so far, and he agreed with me that the mayfly was practically over.

After lunch we sallied forth, and arriving at the part of the road where the waste hatches are situated, could see in the old spot three or four large fish bulging at nymphs, and occasionally taking a winged mayfly, of which there were very few indeed to be seen. I could not persuade my friend to try these fish, as he very candidly told me that they had been hammered day after day by every one of his guests who could manage to cast to them.

In a fit of desperation, I put up a green mayfly male, and was quite prepared to find myself ignominiously beaten by the fish. Selecting the nearest one, I made a first cast, which was a couple of yards short ; on my letting out the requisite amount of line, the second landed just about eighteen inches above the fish's nose. It came like a tiger, was securely hooked, and tore upstream at a pace which was quite alarming. After a time I got on terms with it and worked it down within the range of my vision. Viciously shaking its head, it tried its level best to get through the raised hatch to the waste water, and nothing but the resolute means adopted could have saved the situation. In a few minutes it began to tire, and very soon my friend lifted out of the water in my capacious landing-net a very fine male trout of 3 lbs. 3 oz.

We killed a few good trout and grayling on the Itchen with the brown mayfly, both male and female, during the poor 1903 drake season, but these patterns have not yet scored on the Test in my hands. This is not altogether surprising to me, because in all the years I have collected specimens I never found a single example of any species of *Ephemera* on the Test, except *danica* and the brown mayflies are imitations of *E. vulgata* or *E. lineata*, both of which are found on the Itchen.

One of my few mayfly experiences on the Test in these recent lean years was on the 7th June 1906. It was a fine day, with strongish north-east wind, and there were, for a wonder, a few mayflies. Seeing a fish which appeared of respectable dimensions, I decided to try the green mayfly female—a pattern with which I had not previously killed a sizable fish. The first cast landed right, and up came the fish, but turned out to be a grayling of 2 lbs. exactly.

Of the spent gnat or imitation of the imago, I had a great opportunity of testing the female, as it was my good fortune to be on a stretch of the lower part of the Itchen one day in early June. In the morning there was a strong northerly wind and scarcely any fresh flies hatched out, but about five o'clock the wind dropped, and for the space of at least an hour a great fall of the spent female continued.

The water in question had been fished by twelve experienced and most enthusiastic fishermen, so that the education of the trout was far advanced. It was an ideal reach, deep, slow running, heavily wooded on one bank, and holding a great head of trout and comparatively few grayling, but these generally of large size.

After a few minutes the fish began feeding with great avidity on the flies, which simply covered the surface of the stream from bank to bank, but, as usual, this ravenous consumption of food seemed soon to satisfy their appetites. Trout taking spent may-flies are always prone to come short, and, whether as a result of the caution engendered by being over-fished, or from a peculiar state of the light or reflection on the water, they appeared more particular than usual, and were great adepts at getting lightly hooked and thus making their escape.

By very cautious fishing, and only casting once or twice over each feeding fish, I succeeded in the end in securing a grayling 2 lbs 4 oz., and three trout well over the pound, while my friend, fishing the same pattern, killed one sizable trout and one grayling. The verdict on the new pattern was that it must be considered most satisfactory both as to appearance and killing powers, but it requires more drying and exertion to make it float than the old and celebrated Marryat pattern. This, I believe, is due to the absence of the ribbing hackle, but I do not propose adding it, because it does not seem possible to effect this without diminishing the resemblance of the artificial to the natural insect. It has given the greatest satisfaction to all of my friends who have persevered with it.

The season of 1905 on the Test was a type of what we have had ever since—viz. a very poor show of the mayfly and an abundant hatch of the welshman's button. Of my experiences with this latter fly I shall treat in a subsequent chapter. On the 3rd June in that year we all felt that the mayfly was nearly over, as for three consecutive days there had been no hatch; and as the clouds of amorous males, which in a normal mayfly season should have been seen dancing among the bushes, were conspicuous by their absence, the prospect for the successive seasons looked very poor.

About one o'clock I found a fish rising in the eddy of a deep swirling hole on the main river. A short distance above this deep hole there is an old ford or road of hard gravel over which the main Test, nearly 30 yards wide, flows at a good pace between the banks. Just below this place the river makes a sweep towards the south-east, and about a hundred yards further down contracts, and flows at an even pace for some two to three hundred yards, with a depth of about four to five feet, as is found in a great many other reaches of the river.

On the western bank the stream widens out into a broad bay, and about half the volume of water is turned back into the swirling eddy before referred to. This is from fourteen to sixteen feet deep in the deepest part, and invariably holds a few large and good-conditioned trout. There are two places where the fish rise—one just where the stream flowing down and the outside edge of the eddy flowing up are parallel for some distance, and the other in the full force of the eddy close under the western bank.

The fish in question was rising just at the dividing line of the eddy and the stream, and in such a position a trout invariably wanders about, rising sometimes in the stream with its head in the normal position upstream, and at other times in the eddy with its head turned to what is the usual downstream direction; but of course in this case the natural insects are floating up the eddy towards its mouth The picture, Plate XXVIII., shows this place as seen from the western bank.

The flies on the water were olive, iron-blue, and pale watery duns, and imitations of all these were tried in succession without any response, and after these the male black gnat and spinners of female olive and iron-blue, equally without inducing the fish to rise What with resting the fish, casting at long intervals, and all these changes of fly, it was four

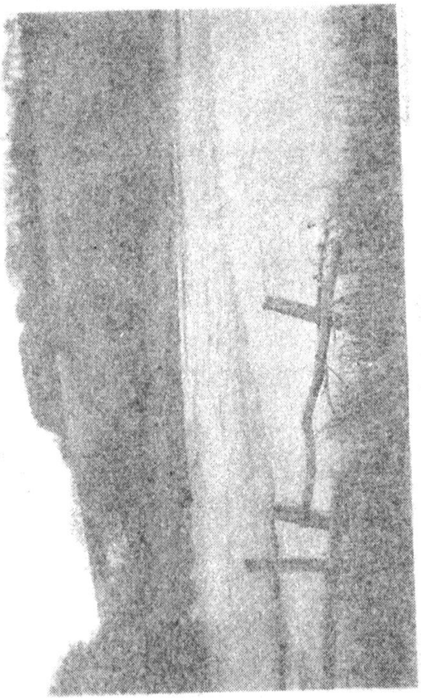

FLY

with a

l in a

t into

water

sferred

n the

good-

re the

wn and

parallel

l horse

feeding

a posi-

etimes

section

th its

direc-

insects

The

n from

ce, and

e were

d after

female

he fish

t long

as tour

pace for some two to three hundred yards, with a
depth of about four to five feet, as is found in a
great many other reaches of the river.

On the western bank the stream widens out into
a broad bay, and about half the volume of water
is turned back into the swirling eddy before referred
to. This is from fourteen to sixteen feet deep in the
deepest part, and invariably holds a few large and good-
conditioned trout. There are two places where the
fish rise—one just where the stream flowing down and
the outside edge of the eddy flowing up are parallel
for some distance, and the other in the full force
of the eddy close under the western bank.

The fish in question was rising just at the dividing
line of the eddy and the stream, and in such a position a fish will be facing sometimes
in the stream with its normal position
upstream, and at other times in the eddy with its
head turned to what is the usual down-stream direction; but of course in this case the natural insects
are floating up the eddy towards its mouth. The
picture, Plate XXVIII, shows this place as seen from
the western bank.

The flies on the water were olive, iron-blue, and
pale watery duns, and imitations of all these were
tried in succession without any response, and after
these the male black gnat and spinners of female
olive and iron-blue, equally without inducing the fish
to rise. What with resting the fish, casting at long
intervals, and all these changes of fly, it was four

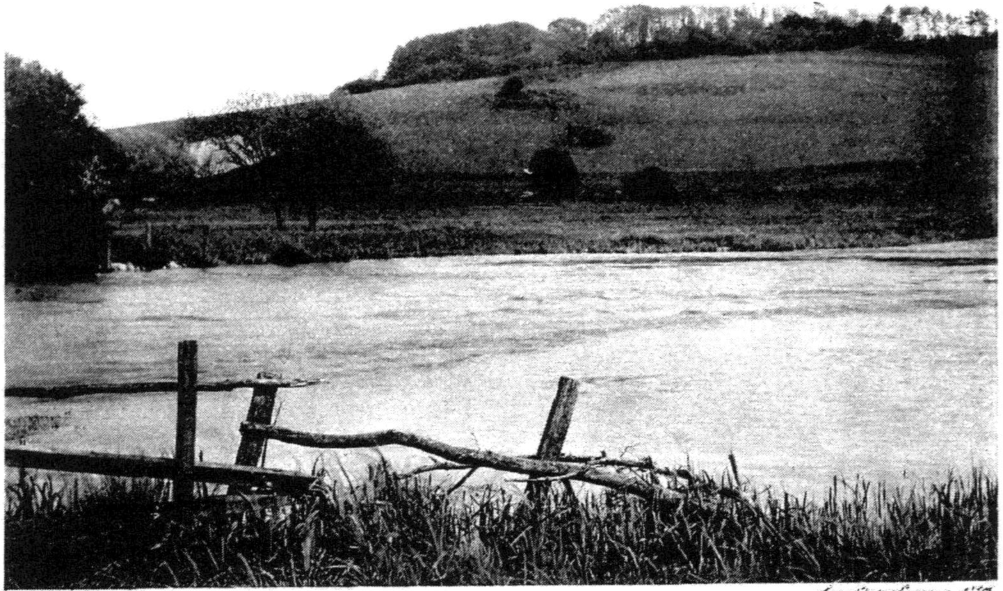

PLATE XXVIII

Swan Electric Engraving Co.

Oakley Hole

o'clock before I put up a male welshman's button.
At the first cast of this fly the fish came short, and
adopting my usual plan, I did not cast a second
time over it with the same fly.

Knowing that fish will often rise at the spent
gnat for some days after it has practically disappeared
from the river, I made up my mind to try one of the
new patterns of it.   While debating whether it should
be the male or the female, I caught sight of a spent
gnat on the surface of the stream, and securing it in
the landing-net, found it was the male.   " Well," said I
to myself, " here goes for the new pattern male spent
gnat!"   After two or three short casts the fly landed
just in front of the fish , it rose leisurely and took it
with equal deliberation.   I slowly raised my hand and
drove the hook home   A furious rush across into the
very strongest of the stream, and a good run of perhaps thirty yards, during which I made the best of my
way downstream, found me with the fish fighting hard
for its life in the smooth water below the hole, and
after the usual tactics of boring down and trying to
entangle me in each weed patch had been frustrated
by strenuous means, the trout—a pretty female of
2 lbs. 1 oz —was duly landed, knocked on the head,
and put into the basket

A long walk upstream, not a rising fish being
visible, wasted another hour, but at length I noticed
one rising about five yards out from and opposite to
a bush on the western bank.   The keeper was with
me, and the first time we saw the rise we both ex-

claimed at the same moment, " That looks like the big fish we saw rising there the week before last." Kneeling down and getting out the correct length of line, after a few attempts I placed the same male spent gnat accurately, and the trout rose at it with the utmost deliberation.

We had been discussing the old question of striking, and whether as a rule one failed to hook fish owing to the action of the hand being too quick or too slow. I was telling him that, personally, I invariably inclined to the theory that one's usual fault is to strike too soon. I was telling him that a very methodical friend of mine, and a past master with the dry fly, said that when a fish rose to his mayfly he invariably counted slowly " One—two—three—four " before striking, but that with the spent gnat he counted "One—two—three—four—five—six," and even then was in no particular hurry to strike.

Being desirous of carrying out this practice, I struck so deliberately that the keeper fancied that I had not seen the rise, so he gently remarked, " That rise is at your fly." I replied, " Yes! I know it was," and then struck. Away went the trout with a dash and a flying leap, and tore about backwards and forwards, up and down, like a creature possessed. After a few minutes of this it plunged head downwards and began jiggering in a very unpleasant manner, but eventually the little 9½-foot rod reduced it to comparative quiet, and the fish was duly landed.

It was so well hooked at the back of the upper jaw that I could not disengage the hook, so I cut off the gut, knocked it on the head, and putting it on the steelyard, found that it weighed just over 3 lbs. 4 oz. On my return home in the evening I tried to cut out the hook, but had eventually to break it off at the bend, as the point was firmly embedded over the barb into one of the small bones of the head. From that day onwards my keeper has never again advocated any method of striking other than the deliberate one.

I will give one more experience of the spent gnat before closing this chapter. In 1907, a season when I had not even tried a mayfly or spent gnat before the 8th June, just after I had finished lunch in the fishing hut on the Oakley stream I saw a fish take a single mayfly. My keeper had gone home to his cottage on some errand, and had left his son, a boy of less than fourteen years of age, with me. I do not think that he had ever landed a big fish before, so I impressed upon him to keep below me, not to lose his head, and to do just what he was told if I hooked the fish.

Out of pure *cussedness* I put up the male spent gnat, although the fish had beyond doubt taken a subimago, and keeping very low, put a long cast well above the spot where the fish rose, and as the wind was light and upstream, it was quite an easy throw to accomplish. The fly floated down, with one of the hackle-point wings out of the water, accurately

over the place, and the fish rose well and was hooked.
It came down towards me at a great pace, and here
again I adopted my usual policy in such cases of
slacking to the fish and quietly reeling up the line
so as not to have any loose coils hanging about.

The moment I tightened, the trout tore downstream, and I after it and past it. It paused, and
then again bore away downstream, and once more I
raced down and got below it This was repeated
several times, until at length we were quite two
hundred yards below the place where the trout was
hooked I looked round for the boy and the net,
and, to my agreeable surprise, he was about ten yards
below me waiting my instructions I told him to put
his net in the water and sink it well, and gradually
worked the trout into the landing-net, and in another
moment a splendidly conditioned female trout of
3 lbs 3 oz. was on the bank.

That boy never forgot his lesson, and since then
he has been learning a keeper's work under his father.
He has landed literally scores and scores of big fish
for my friends as well as myself, and we are unani-
mous in declaring that we would as soon trust him
with the landing-net when playing a big fish as any
keeper in the county of Hampshire. I venture to
predict that there is every likelihood of his becoming
as good a keeper as his father, who, to my mind,
is one of the best I have ever seen.

Referring to the paucity of mayflies nowadays, it
just occurs to me that the plan adopted by my old

friend, the late Major Turle, might perhaps be of interest as showing how he did succeed in inducing fish to come on the rise at the mayfly or spent gnat. A part of his water at Newton Stacey included a narrow, deep, and comparatively slow-running stream generally known as the Black Ditch. About half-way down this carrier was a bridge crossing it, and as the trout in this ditch were among the very largest and gamest in the Test, and they only came on the rise at spent gnat or sedges, he thought out and adopted the following tactics.

In the morning he would send his keeper out to collect a great number of the imagines of both sexes and keep them alive in a basket. Towards evening he would station the keeper on the bridge and, making a wide circuit so as not to show himself, take up his position some fifty or sixty yards below. The keeper would take an imago from the basket, and having first given it a pinch on the head to make it appear spent, would drop it in the water.

At intervals he would repeat this, and sooner or later a few of the big fish would commence feeding on the flies as they floated down. Turle would mark down most accurately the spot where the big fish were rising, and as soon as one came fairly on the feed, would put his artificial spent gnat once or twice over the trout.

He was pre-eminently good with the mayfly or spent gnat, and all round a very fine dry-fly fisherman, and he has often told me that by this method he has secured some of the very best fish he ever killed. Of course at times the fish in the Black Ditch took spent gnat without any of this *dodging* (if I may call it so), and Marryat loved the place. The fish were very difficult to rise, and terrifying when hooked, and the great master himself told me that on one June day many years ago he was utterly smashed up by nine consecutive fish he hooked, all monsters, although he was fishing with the stoutest and strongest gut he possessed.

I wish it to be clearly understood that I do not in any way recommend my readers to adopt this dodge. In the first instance, I doubt whether it can be deemed fair fly-fishing, and in the second, I am quite convinced that if it should be practised on any large scale it would very soon defeat its own object, and only serve to make the fish even more shy and more disinclined to take the fly than they were before.

I have, however, diverged from my subject, which was to suggest that if any of our good friends should try this experiment on their own water of feeding the fish with the natural mayfly or spent gnat with a view of ascertaining whether this will bring them on the rise when the hatch is not very great, their success is not likely to be in any way permanent. I fear, too, that in addition to laying themselves open to a charge of "ground baiting," they may be accused of decreasing (even the harmless entomologist with his bottles has not escaped calumny in this respect!) the breeding stock of mayflies for subsequent years, and thus perhaps helping to advance the date when the glories of the drake will have departed and *Ephemera* be altogether a thing of the past, possibly regarded by our successors as a myth, and all our histories of sport with it as " Fish Tails."

CHAPTER III

OLIVE, PALE WATERY, AND IRON-BLUE DUNS

THE duns are undoubtedly the most important patterns of artificial flies during the day in the spring, late summer, and autumn. The olives are at once the earliest in date, and continue more or less *en évidence* throughout the year. The iron blue is the immediate successor of the olives, and on the Test is often preferred to the olives by the fish when both are present. From, say, the third week in April until the end of the fishing season it may be looked for on most days, and certainly for the Test should be considered the predominant form of floating insect food for the trout and grayling in the daytime, excepting during the fortnight when the mayfly formerly did, and the welshman's button nowadays does, seem to exercise a fatal fascination for the fish.

The iron-blue is less plentiful on the Itchen than on the Test, and is therefore not so favourite a pattern in the former stream as on the latter. To compensate for this, the pale watery dun—the first appearance of which is due towards the end of May—may often be considered a likely fly to rise a feeding trout in the daytime or early evening when it is on the water. As far as my personal experience goes, this fly has not proved a very killing one on the Test, although at times it has been found deadly on days when neither the olive nor the iron-blue have been of any use.

To extract from the diary all the occasions since 1903 when duns have been successful would be in effect to copy out the records of every time the fish rose well during the hours of daylight. I will therefore only cite a few examples, and suggest the well-known adage, *Ex uno disce omnes.*

In the early part of 1904, when in treaty for the Test water I am now fishing, I was invited to take a friend over on a date to be named by the then tenant, who fixed upon the 3rd May. On our arrival at the water we found that it was a rough and inclement day, with passing showers, northerly to north-westerly wind, and transient bright intervals. The only fly on the stream was the olive, but during the morning hours the hatch was so sparse that very few fish were rising. From about one to three o'clock the state of things improved a little, and spasmodically sufficient olive duns were present to tempt an occasional trout to take an odd fly. Before this time I had collected a few specimens, and after full examination had established to my satisfaction the fact that, as I had anticipated, the olive dun of the Test was identical in size, shape, colour, and in every detail revealed by a glass of moderate magnification, with its brother of the Itchen.

During the rise very few of the fish were taking the floating insect, and those bulging did not respond

to my occasional invitation. With a male olive I
landed one pretty fish of 1 lb. 4 oz., and joined my
friend at an *al fresco* lunch fully persuaded that the
rise was over for the day. He reported that he had
hooked three trout but that they were coming very
short, and he had therefore only landed one of
them, of exactly 2 lbs., a perfect fish of the High
Wycombe type, *i e.* short, thick, silvery, and with black
spots, but with few if any red ones. After lunch he
proceeded upstream to explore the top meadow of
the beat, while I settled down to the enjoyment of
the landscape and a peaceful pipe.

Presently the keeper and I at the same moment
saw a quiet rise in the smooth water at the edge of
a rough run immediately above us, and just within
my reach. A few minutes before I had taken a dun
off the water and identified it as a female olive, so I
promptly put up one of this pattern. The first cast
came off; the fish rose, was hooked, and after a few
minutes of hard play I rolled the trout headlong down
over a short shallow, keeping on the move myself so
as to be well below the fish.

As the keeper was a stranger to me, I asked him
if he was afraid of netting a big fish on this very
shallow water, and although his reply was a brisk
and cheery one, yet I felt somewhat anxious. I was,
however, quite reassured on noting his deliberate and
confident handling of the landing-net, and was even
better satisfied when, by a very smart bit of work,
he quietly netted the fish and laid it on the bank. A

tap on the head, and a fine male trout of 3 lbs. 7 oz. lay dead on the ground, and was placed in the basket.

The keeper then slowly made his way downstream to try and spot another feeding fish, while I returned to the place from which I had cast to the trout first killed. About four or five yards above the spot where the big male fish had taken my artificial, I saw another very quiet rise, and waited for a long time in vain to make quite sure of the exact locale. Being fairly certain of the position, at length I decided to chance it, and two or three casts were made with the same fly, when once more there was a slow and deliberate rise, and an equally slow and deliberate wrist action in striking drove the barb well home in another good trout.

This fish simply ripped across the river with a long jump to the other bank and played very hard, but I kept working it downstream until I found in a deeply indented bay on my side of the river a favourable place to net it. The fish was gradually worked in, and we saw, swimming deeply down in the water, a very pretty silvery trout of good size. Gradually I managed to force it up to the surface of the water, and another efficient bit of work with the landing-net secured this, a female of 2 lbs. 8 oz.

Presently my friend returned and reported that he had not seen a fish rising well within the limits of the fishery, and added that he had tried every one that had shown at all with a succession of the old standard patterns, and could not get the faintest response from any of them. I may confess that my happier experience was most gratifying to me and flattering to the new pattern.

Another instance of success with this fly receives pictorial demonstration in Plate XXIX., the photograph of a female trout, 1 lb. 9 oz., killed on the main Test, by my good friend Martin E. Mosely. It is given here as the representation of what I consider the most symmetrical and best marked Test trout I have ever seen.

One morning in the middle of April I had occupied an hour or two of the forenoon in inspecting a neighbouring fishery, and at 12.30 found myself on the main Test. It was a bitterly cold day, with north-north-east wind, and very rough, and according to all the *dicta* of the wiseacres of olden times it was "far too cold for any duns to hatch." Nevertheless, at about 1 15 P.M. the olives began to show, and for about an hour there appeared one of the very best hatches of duns it has ever been my fortune to witness.

The fish generally were bulging, an expression the meaning of which all my readers no doubt fully understand. They were, in fact, actively engaged in darting at and securing under water the nymphs swimming to the surface, there to split open the nymphal envelope and emerge as a winged subimago or dun. Now and again fish feeding in this way will follow the nymph to the surface, and if the winged fly should just at this moment escape from the shuck the trout will rise at

response from any of them. I may confess that my happier experience was most gratifying to me and flattering to the new pattern.

Another instance of success with this fly receives pictorial demonstration in Plate XXIX., the photograph of a female trout, 1 lb. 5 oz. killed on the main Test, by my good friend Martin E. Mosely. It is given here as the representation of what I consider the most symmetrical and best marked Test trout I have ever seen.

One morning in the middle of April I had occupied an hour or two of the forenoon in inspecting a neighbouring fishery, and at 12.30 found myself on the main Test. It was a bitterly cold day, with north-north-east wind and very rough, and resolving to all the tradition the whereabouts of olden time I went .... hatch." Now .... begun to hatch and .... appeared one of the very best hatches of duns it has ever been my fortune to witness.

The fish generally were bulging, an expression the meaning of which all my readers no doubt fully understand. They were, in fact, actively engaged in darting at and securing under water the nymphs swimming to the surface, there to split open the nymphal envelope and emerge as a winged subimago or dun. Now and again fish feeding in this way will follow the nymph to the surface, and if the winged fly should ...... at this moment escape from the shuck the trout will rise at

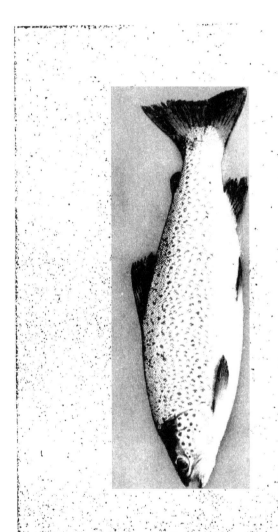

PLATE XXIX.

A Perfect Seaside Trout 1 lb. 9 oz.

Swan Electric Engraving Co.

and take it. It is therefore not altogether surprising that a bulging fish should occasionally make a mistake and annex the floating pattern, if it should just be over its nose at the psychological moment. It is, however, generally bad policy to keep on hammering away at a bulging fish, and as a rule more profitable to go farther afield and discover a fish indulging in the legitimate pursuit of the floating subimago.

On the day in question the direction of the wind—north-north-east—was downstream and towards the bank of the stream on which I was located, and as only the western bank is included in the estate, I could not cross the river. This is perhaps the most difficult wind to circumvent, but, unless it is very violent, with a comparatively short cast and the downward cut the fly can be put into the wind and over the rising fish. It must be remembered that to cast against the wind there must be no acceleration in the timing and no increase in the force used—in fact, the golfer's adage, " Slow back and do not press," quite succinctly describes the advice to be given to the dry-fly tyro.

A fish rising in mid-water was seen to take a dun, and a careful and accurate cast put the fly, the female olive, perfectly in position. The fish took, and after the usual tussle was duly netted, a good Test trout, which turned the scales at 2 lbs. 15 oz., a male in ideal condition Some time later a fish rising shyly under my own bank took a floating insect, and after a few attempts again the same fly was over its nose, taken, and a second male of 1 lb. 9 oz. was landed.

It was then 3 o'clock, and I felt fairly certain that the rise was over for the day. I therefore started to walk back to the fishing hut, which was situated on another stream about half a mile away.

When I reached the upper part of this stream I waited for a few moments, because there were one or two olives floating down under the opposite—the leeward—bank. A single bubble and the disappearance of a dun indicated the presence of another rising fish, and the same fly was again despatched across the river to float over the spot where the natural insect had just been taken. Again there was a quiet rise, and again striking slowly I found another good fish tearing downstream as if possessed by some evil spirit. Strong pressure and a fully bowed rod checked its wild career, and a moving bar of silver in the air gave the cue to drop the rod point as the trout flung itself out of the water. This was an exceptionally strong and active trout and took a long time to kill, so that by the time it was in the net and its weight and sex ascertained (a female of 2 lbs. 13 oz.) the day's fishing was positively at an end. Not so bad for a short April day—three trout, 7 lbs. 5 oz., and all killed on the female olive!

The female olive played a distinguished part on what was, to my mind, quite a remarkable day. The May morning was very rough, with southerly wind and rain falling—in fact, about as unpleasant a day as could be imagined. The water was ruffled in the most sheltered parts, and in the exposed ones

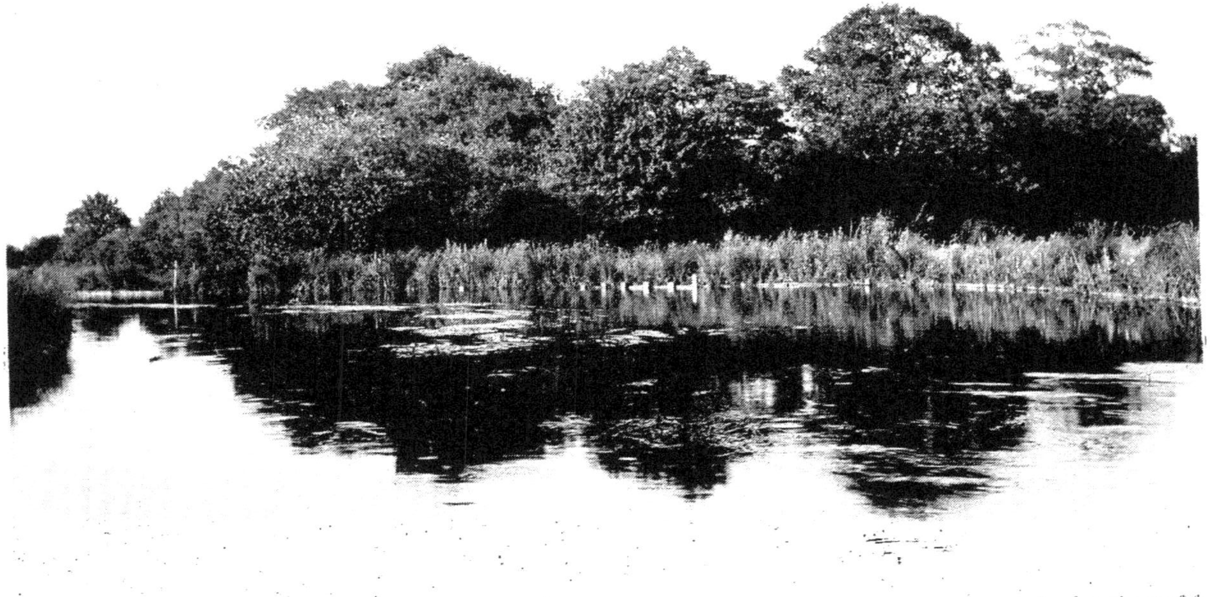

PLATE XXX

Swan Electric Engraving Co. Ltd

A Still Reach of the Oakley Stream.

there were quite high waves. The hatch of fly was very sparse, and it was not surprising that few rising fish could be seen. Starting from the hut, the keeper and I walked along upstream, looking at every likely spot, and naturally our eyes were all on the water. The keeper was the first to discern a rise, and as soon as I could locate it accurately a female olive was placed over the fish, and it was just understood was landed, and removed. The photograph in Plate XXX. is a pleasant reminder of the place and of several exciting events which happened mysteriously afterwards.

A little higher up another fish rose, took the fly, and was duly landed, a male, 2 lbs. 1 oz. A few yards higher up a second was killed, a female, 1 lb. 7 oz. Then again a few yards still higher up I got another female of 1 lb. 9 oz. We were then at a point a short distance below a plank bridge, and in some deadish water in the middle of the river a fish rose and gave us the impression of being a big one. It was not an easy place to fish, because there was a fair run on each side of the slack water and the fish rose several times in succession, but always in the smooth wedge.

However, "nothing venture, nothing have," and with plenty of slack line the fly was once more put fairly and squarely before the fish. A nose broke the surface of the water, and the next moment the hooked fish ran upstream, and could not be checked before it was quite six or seven yards above the plank

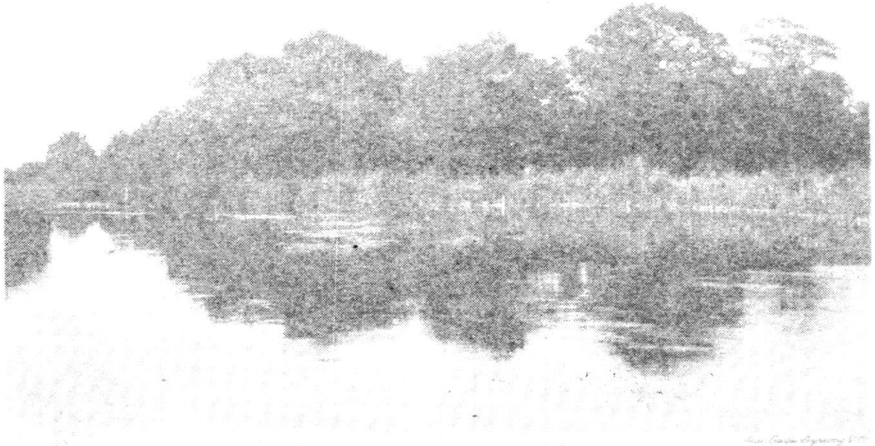

A Fair Reach of the Winding Stream

there were quite high waves. The hatch of fly was
very sparse, and it was not surprising that few rising
fish could be seen. Starting from the hut, the keeper
and I walked along upstream, halting at every likely
spot, and naturally our eyes were all on the water.
The keeper was the first to discern a rise, and as soon
as I could locate it accurately a female olive was
placed over the fish, and a trout just undersized was
landed, and returned. The photograph in Plate
XXX. is a pleasant reminder of the place and of
several exciting events which happened immediately
afterwards.

A little higher up another fish rose, took the fly,
and was duly landed, a male, 2 lbs. 1 oz A few yards
higher up a second was killed, a female, 1 lb 7 oz.
Then again a few yards still higher up I got another
female of 1 lb. 9 oz. We were then at a point a
short distance below a plank bridge, and in some
deadish water in the middle of the river a fish rose
and gave us the impression of being a big one. It
was not an easy place to fish, because there was a
fair run on each side of the slack water and the
fish rose several times in succession, but always in
the smooth wedge.

However, "nothing venture, nothing have," and
with plenty of slack line the olive was once more put
fairly and squarely before the fish. A nose broke
the surface of the water, and the next moment the
hooked fish ran upstream, and could not be checked
before it was quite six or seven yards above the plank

bridge. It then turned, came down at express speed, and leaped high into the air. The moment it was back in the stream it tore across to the opposite bank, jumped again, then began working downstream with its tail up and its head down, trying to bore down and probably entangle the line in the weeds. If a fish like this is well hooked, and if the fisherman does not lose his head, the result can be safely predicted, and in this case a lovely fish, a female of just over 3 lbs., was added to the bag. A strange circumstance in connection with this day was that although a great majority of the natural insects on the water were iron-blues, yet every sizable feeding fish came well and fastened to the olive.

As we turned to go downstream another fish rose below us, and as it would not come to an olive the fly was changed to a female iron-blue, and another fish just under the sizable limit of 1¼ lbs was returned. It was then one o'clock, and as we had not left the hut until after 11 30, had hooked and landed every fish we had seen rising, and killed two brace aggregating 8 lbs 1 oz., I think the day can fairly be described as ideal.

Not perhaps ideal but gratifying was an April morning when I arrived at the river-side at about 10.30, and putting up a female olive, had just begun to anoint it with paraffin, when a quiet rise on the inside edge of a run over a little shallow patch in the centre of the main river attracted my attention. Walking a few paces up and dropping on my knees, as

A Brace of Sea Trout
Male 2 lb 5 oz   Female 2 lb 8 oz

the bank was very high at this part of the river, I
gradually crawled into position, and letting out sufficient line to cover the fish, placed the fly to the left
of the spot where it had just risen. Quickly recovering and drying the fly, it landed just right at the
next attempt, and the trout came, but did not make a
very determined fight of it, especially as it was no
small fish, in good condition—2 lbs. 5 oz.

It was then past eleven o'clock, and seeing nothing
rising above, I strolled down to the next meadow,
where another fish put up. The female olive was
offered to it, but meeting with no response, I changed
to the male olive, and at the first cast the trout rose
and was promptly killed, a male of 1 lb. 13 oz. Not
another rise was seen during that day, but it was a
goodly brace.

Another big April fish was caught on a rough,
dull day with southerly to south-westerly wind.
Nearly all the flies on the water were dark olives,
so I put up one of the female dark olives and
killed one of the many abnormally short and handsome fish I have taken from the Test, weighing 5 lbs.
1 oz. Plate XXXI. scarcely does it justice.

Yet another April memory. It was a bitterly
cold day, with east-north-east wind blowing quite
freshly, and although there was a fair rise of fish,
I could do nothing with either the male or female
olive. After a late lunch at the riverside I caught
a dun and found that it was a dark olive male, so
put up the imitation of this. The first fish I cast

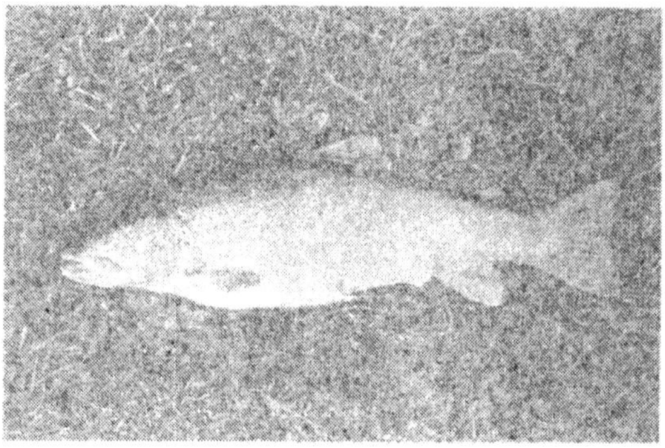

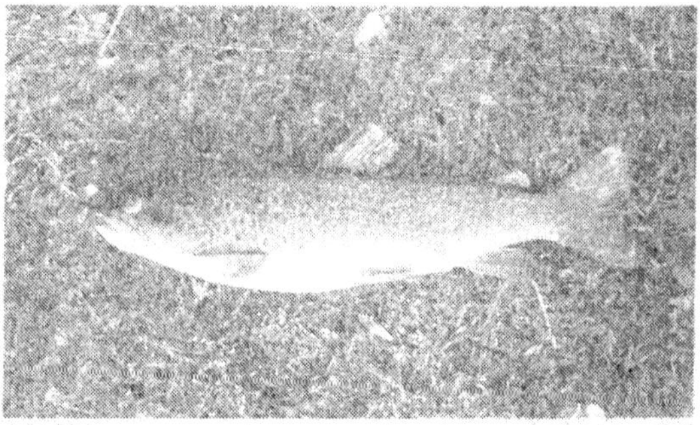

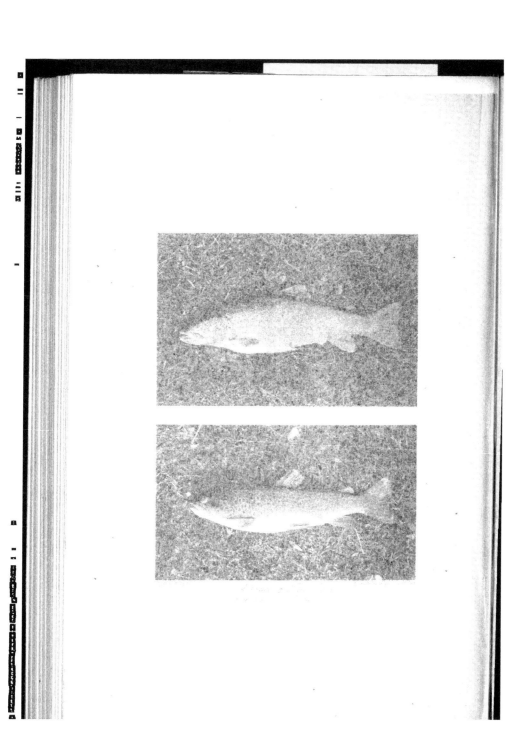

the bank was very high at this part of the river, I gradually crawled into position, and letting out sufficient line to cover the fish, placed the fly to the left of the spot where it had just risen. Quickly recovering and drying the fly, it landed just right at the next attempt, and the trout came, but did not make a very determined fight of it, especially as it was no small fish, in good condition—3 lbs. 3 oz.

It was then past eleven o'clock, and seeing nothing rising above, I strolled down to the next meadow, where another fish put up The female olive was offered to it, but meeting with no response, I changed to the male olive, and at the first cast the trout rose and was promptly killed, a male of 1 lb. 13 oz. Not another rise was seen during that day, but it was a goodly brace.

Another big April fish was caught on a rough, dull day with southerly to south-westerly wind. Nearly all the flies on the water were dark olives, so I put up one of the female dark olives and killed one of the many abnormally short and handsome fish I have taken from the Test, weighing 3 lbs. 1 oz. Plate XXXI. scarcely does it justice.

Yet another April memory. It was a bitterly cold day, with east-north-east wind blowing quite freshly, and although there was a fair rise of duns, I could do nothing with either the male or female olive. After a late lunch at the river-side I caught a dun and found that it was a dark olive male, so put up the imitation of this. The first fish I cast over came at it and was killed, a male of 2 lbs. 14 oz., and then in quick succession I landed and returned three other trout all between $1\frac{1}{4}$ lbs. and $1\frac{1}{2}$ lbs., the latter being the limit I had imposed on my guests and myself for that season.

Mayday 1909 belied its poetic reputation, being rough, with heavy showers of sleet and occasional snow, and the wind was as near as possible due north. For about three-quarters of an hour there was a fair show of dark olives, but the fish were rising badly, and taking even worse. I would urge that such a day is a supreme test of the efficacy of the patterns, and I was very pleased to kill a brace of fish with the female dark olive dun between two and three o'clock. The smaller fish was a female of 1 lb. 4 oz., and the larger a male of 2 lbs. 8 oz., and in Plate XXXI. the photograph of this fish is reproduced.

An intimation was conveyed to me by a mutual friend that an old acquaintance, well advanced in years but still keen for sport, would be staying within a few miles of my headquarters during the latter days of an earlier May. An invitation to join me for a day's fishing was cordially accepted, and on the morning of the appointed day the veteran turned up, just as the first after-breakfast pipe was fairly lighted. A short yarn while donning waders and loading rods, tackle, lunch, and all other necessaries into a trap to convey the party to the river-side, was convincing evidence that eighty-three summers had not sufficed to cool my friend's ardour or take the rough edge off his appetite for fly-fishing.

The scene of action was a by-stream which flows out of the main river at a point about three miles above the upper boundary, and rejoins the Test proper about a mile below the lower boundary of the fishery. The upper part of this—the Oakley—stream is smooth running, and in many parts comparatively deep; in fact, on a small scale typical of the main Test, the very best of Hampshire chalk streams For about half a mile its character is quite changed, there being a steep downward declivity, causing a series of rapid, rough runs over boulders which are only a few inches under water when the stream is at its normal summer level.

A stranger suddenly deposited on this part of the river would never imagine that he was in the south· country, where the sizable trout averaged nearly 2 lbs. in weight, but would compare it in his mind with a Scotch or Welsh mountain stream where the fish would on a favourable day perhaps run three or four to the pound. The weather was ideal, a southerly wind perhaps rather too strong, and a beautiful, bright, hot, sunny day ; the mayfly was just beginning to hatch out, but as usual *Salmo fario* had not at this early part of the hatch discovered its palatable nature.

A careful scrutiny of the flies on the water showed that the olive and iron-blue duns were present, and the spinners (male and female) of these two species of the genus *Baetis* were dancing about in the air.

An iron-blue was patiently tried over feeding fish without effect, and after a time a female olive was mounted in its place. The wind was across the stream, the sedges on the bank and the grass in the meadow were very high, and altogether the conditions were to a considerable extent baffling. It was, therefore, not surprising that the octogenarian soon began to tire, and he begged me try and hook one of the fish and let him have the pleasure of playing and killing it.

The very first cast was successful, and the rod was immediately handed over to him, with an injunction to be careful as it was a big fish. It played hard and deep, and after a longish fight came up to the surface for a moment before dashing down again. This moment, however, sufficed to show the prominent opalescent dorsal fin of a grayling of nearly 3 lbs. Just as the keeper lowered his net into the water the fish made one last desperate dive, and the hook came away.

My old friend handed the rod back to me with a subdued and saddened air, and after we had returned an undersized trout, our attention was directed to what was evidently a good fish rising in a quiet smooth patch between two heavy runs, an attractive but difficult place pictured in Plate XXXII.

Some little preliminary study of the position was necessary, because it is never easy to float a fly over such a place without drag. Once I had settled down at the right place and had begun with a very

' FLY

ing fish
live was
ross the
grass in
the con-
It was,
an soon
k one of
ying and

the rod
n injunc-
t played
came up
g down
how the
ying of
net into
live, and

me with
had re-
directed
a quiet
attractive

ison was
ly over
settled
th a very

An iron-blue was patiently tried over feeding fish without effect, and after a time a female olive was mounted in its place. The wind was across the stream, the sedges on the bank and the grass in the meadow were very high, and altogether the conditions were to a considerable extent baffling. It was, therefore, not surprising that the octogenarian soon began to tire, and he begged me try and hook one of the fish and let him have the pleasure of playing and killing it.

The very first cast was successful, and the rod was immediately handed over to him, with an injunction to be careful as it was a big fish. It played hard and strong, and after a toughish fight came up to the surface for a moment before dashing down again. This moment however sufficed to show the prominent opalescent spot and a reading of nearly 3 lbs. As the fish made its last desperate dive, and the hook came away.

My old friend handed the rod back to me with a subdued and saddened air, and after we had returned an undersized trout, our attention was directed to what was evidently a good fish rising in a quiet smooth patch between two heavy runs, an attractive but difficult place pictured in Plate XXXII.

Some little preliminary study of the position was necessary, because it is never easy to float a fly over such a place without drag. Once I had settled down at the right place and had begun with a very

PLATE XXXII

The River below the Bridge

slack line, the olive was seen travelling steadily, quite dry and cocked, over the feeding fish. The typical, deliberate rise of a large Test trout followed, and the equally typical, slow, steady strike drove the hook home.

Without a moment's hesitation, the trout went forty yards upstream, turned to the right, to the left, up, down, across, and at each check tried its hardest to get into the weeds. Never for a second did it stop or give the fisherman an instant for consideration. Each time I tried to stop it or turn it, another head-long rush took line off the reel and made me follow the fish for fear of its getting out of hand.

My plan with a heavy trout is invariably to try and bully it, but this was quite impossible, as the harder I tried to hold it the faster it ran. Never do I remember to have seen a trout tear about in the mad way that this one did, and gradually we worked some eighty or a hundred yards below the point where it was hooked. All this time the fish was above the fisherman, but suddenly it tore down over some rough boulders forming a kind of weir about six inches under the surface.

Once more I got below it, and thought it must soon give in. Another rush downstream, and I found myself a short distance above a place where it was not possible to follow the fish lower down, owing to the presence of a large oak leaning over the water. The trunk of this tree was too big for me to be able to pass the rod round it, even with the keeper's

I

assistance, and the depth of the water, quite 5 feet, rendered it undesirable, or even dangerous, to try wading in so strong a current. Once I managed to work the trout upstream until it was just above the tree-trunk, but instantly it dashed down again, and the keeper, with the net below the tree, could not quite reach it. We could all see the fish for a few seconds, a perfect specimen of about 3 lbs. in weight, but, alas! back came the hook, and we were beaten.

Plate XXXIII shows this obstructive oak leaning over the stream, taken from below. Larger trout I have often killed, but never have I seen a fish to approach in activity and speed that lost trout, which certainly for at least seven minutes tore backwards and forwards at its top speed without a single check, and all that can be said is that it deserved its liberty.

There is nothing very extraordinary in one's rising and hooking fish and their going on feeding as if nothing had happened. In "An Angler's Auto-biography," pages 101 and 102, there is a quotation from a *Field* article of the late Francis Francis in which he described in most humorous terms how Marryat, fishing over a feeding Test trout, left his fly in its mouth. The fish continued rising, so Francis had a turn at it, and the trout rose at his fly. After a few moments it began rising again as fast as ever, and Marryat once more put his fly over it and again tempted it. This went on until eventually one of them got hung up in a post just above where the

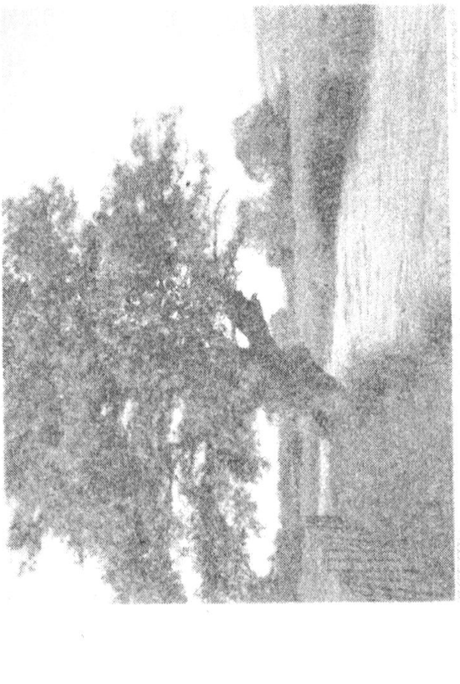

assistance, and the depth of the water, quite 5 feet, rendered it undesirable, or even dangerous, to try wading in so strong a current. Once I managed to work the trout upstream until it was just above the tree-trunk, but instantly it dashed down again, and the keeper, with the net below the tree, could not quite reach it. We could all see the fish for a few seconds, a perfect specimen of about 3 lbs. in weight, but, alas! back came the hook, and we were beaten.

Plate XXXIII. shows this obstructive oak leaning over the stream, taken from below. Larger trout I have often killed, but never have I seen a fish to approach in activity and speed that lost trout, which possibly for about seven minutes tore backwards and forwards at top speed without a single check, and all that can be said is that it deserved its liberty.

There is nothing very extraordinary in one's rising and hooking fish and their going on feeding as if nothing had happened. In "An Angler's Autobiography," pages 101 and 102, there is a quotation from a *Field* article of the late Francis Francis in which he described in most humorous terms how Marryat, fishing over a feeding Test trout, left his fly in its mouth. The fish continued rising, so Francis had a turn at it, and the trout rose at his fly. After a few moments it began rising again as fast as ever, and Marryat once more put his fly over it and again tempted it. This went on until eventually one of them got hung up in a post just above where the

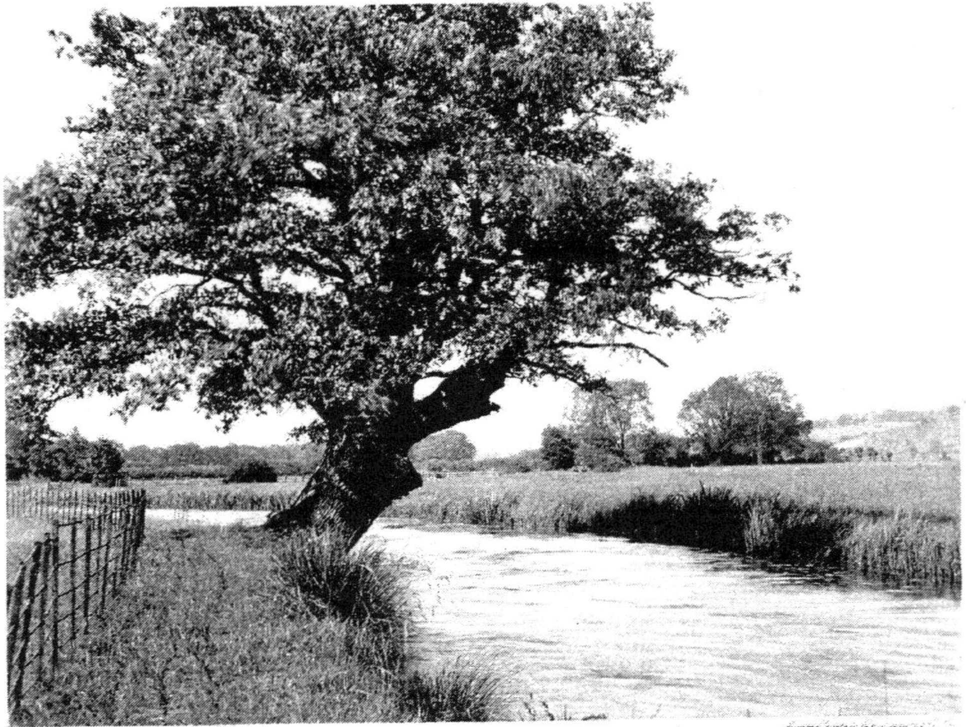

PLATE XXXIII

The Leaning Oak

fish was feeding, and not wishing to leave half his cast there, Marryat went across and scared the fish while disentangling his tackle from the post

In another *Field* article published on 21st April 1883, Francis Francis, writing of a day at Houghton when he was staying with me, says· "I got one tidy one 2½ lbs. on North Head, who gave grand sport, and I lost one or two and got out some undersized ones The fish were very *pernickity*, but I had an adventure worth noting with one. Just above North Head, where the river is going on for thirty yards wide, there were two fish rising under the bank, about a yard or so out. I knew they were pretty good ones, and I tried them again and again, but could not quite reach them for the strong downstream wind. My friend, however, had a longer rod than mine—a fifteen-footer or young grilse rod cut down—and he offered it to me. With this I put a fly across very easily, and the first fish came, but, the rod being heavier and stiffer than mine, I left half the cast in him.

"'Never mind,' I said, 'there's the other fish rising ; tie on another fly and let us get him ' Another of the same flies was on in a twinkling, the cast made, and the fish on, and I got him out—a handsome 1½ lb. fish. My friend went to take out the fly, when 'Hallo!' he said, 'why, it's the same fish ; for here's the other fly, side by side with this one, and with the yard of gut hanging to it.' I have often taken fish half-an-hour after with another fly and with only a foot of gut, but here was a fish caught within five or six minutes with a yard of gut hanging to him and the very same fly. My own opinion is that the feat is unexampled, I never heard of such a case before."

The following episode is to my mind even more curious, the more so that it occurred twice within a few minutes. I had wasted all the morning on a part of the main Test, where the weeds were coming down so thickly as to make fishing most unpleasant, if not impossible. Strange to say, for this season, 1908, the then newly formed Test and Itchen Trout Fishing Association had issued a circular requesting all proprietors and lessees of water on those rivers to abstain from cutting weeds between the 15th May and 15th June. The result of this circular was that weed-cutting was in full swing on the 18th May, and the river was absolutely unfishable!

After lunch I walked over to the Oakley stream, and after wandering about for nearly an hour, had not seen a sizable fish rising, although occasional olive and iron-blue duns came sailing down. At length, on a very rapid run, a fish came to the surface and took some floating insect. After I had made a few careful casts with the iron-blue dun male it rose, fairly to the fly, was hooked, ran across the river, and the hook came away.

Every movement of the trout could be followed, and it returned at once to its original position, and, after a brief interval, resumed its interrupted meal.

A change was made to an olive dun male, and again the fish rose, and this time fastened. In accordance with my usual method of dealing with a large trout, I at once turned its head downstream and towed it along for quite sixty yards It seemed quite bewildered, came down quietly to the net, was landed, duly and justly admired, and weighed 2 lbs. 12 oz.

Proceeding a short distance upstream to a broad shallow, I espied another rising fish; the male olive dun was put over it, and it came short. Something prompted me to change to the iron-blue dun male, but it would not rise again. Some four or five yards farther out in the stream, another and apparently somewhat larger fish was seen to rise.

At the first cast it took the iron-blue dun, tore across the water, forged upstream, turned downstream again, and just as it reached the spot where it had risen the hook came away. After a few minutes the trout settled down to rise in its old position, and then, breaking off the iron-blue, I knotted on the same male olive, put it over the fish, and killed it —a female of exactly 2 lbs.

Thus, one after another, both these fish were hooked on the iron-blue, gave a good run, got away, returned to their respective stations, and fell victims to the charms of the olive dun male.

The pale watery duns are patterns which, as has been before remarked, have in my hands proved far more deadly on the Itchen than on the Test. During

1903 and 1904, in the months of May, June, and July, I had very good sport in the St. Cross and other Itchen waters with both sexes of this fly, and since then on odd days occasional fish have succumbed to their fate, tempted by these patterns, on the Test, but my experience does not tempt me to dwell on them at any length.

With the iron-blue it is another story. The female, for instance, was successful on the 16th May 1907 in killing four trout of 7 lbs. 3 oz, and the male on the 20th May in the same year secured a brace weighing 4 lbs. 8 oz. in the hands of a friend of mine, a very good fisherman, and one of the cheeriest of companions. On the 9th May in the same year I killed 2½ brace of trout with the male iron-blue, weighing 8 lbs. 12 oz., returning another and getting broken in a good fish.

The iron-blue is a good autumn pattern, and I have done quite well with it from time to time. One of the latest entries in my diary records a brace, 3 lbs. 8 oz, killed early in September with the male.

The iron-blue once made an interesting capture for me of a debatable trout. During the early part of 1906 I often used to go down to the lowest point of the water on the main river, and frequently saw a large fish rising just opposite to the fence dividing this meadow from the next. A friend and neighbour who was the proprietor of this meadow just below my boundary would often lean over the fence and have a chat with me while waiting for the rise. We often admired this trout, and in a chaffing spirit I told him that some days it was my fish and some days his. He freely gave me permission to cast to it even when below the boundary fence, but I set myself the task of trying to kill it on one of the rare occasions when it had taken up its position at a point unmistakably above the boundary.

From early April to the middle of June my neighbour often tried this fish, but I do not honestly think I had put three casts over it, and we had both reluctantly arrived at the conclusion that it was likely to live to another season. On the 29th June, a cold day, generally dull, but with occasional gleams of sunshine and a hard north-easterly wind, I had been out all the morning, and do not think that my patience had been rewarded by the sight of an honest rise of any sort. Just before one o'clock I decided to walk once more down to the boundary fence, and if I could see nothing rising, purposed taking my simple lunch and returning to the fishing hut.

In an airy manner, and without any notion of such a thing happening, I remarked to the keeper that the big one would certainly be rising and that it was equally certain that we should kill it—the more so as my neighbour below was not out that day, and hence had not thrown over it and made it shy. On my arrival at the fence, sure enough it was rising well above the boundary; the fly on the cast, a female iron-blue, was promptly placed before its nose, and as promptly taken. The trout made its way rapidly downstream, and although my neighbour is too good a sportsman to have in any way objected to my trespassing on his land when following it, I had made up my mind to kill this fish without going below the fence. All went well, and a handsome male trout of 3 lbs. 2 oz. was killed and despatched to a London friend the same afternoon.

I fancy that I can hear the critical or sceptical reader remark that throughout this chapter there is an unbroken record of successful days He would ask : " Does the author never fail ? Are his vaunted new patterns always irresistible ? Does not he, like the rest of us, have his unfortunate and disappointing days ? " My answer is a simple one : I have as many disappointing days as any of my readers, perhaps more. I fail continually. I leave flies in the fish's mouth ; I am weeded and broken. Some evenings I get home dead beat, tired out, depressed, and ready to declare that I will give up dry-fly fishing altogether. I hope, however, that I have learnt to look at sport from the optimistic point of view, and so the next morning I wake up keener than ever, and once more sally forth to the river resolved to do or die.

An anecdote with which I will conclude this chapter will give the reader the opinion of the great master of dry fly on the efficacy of particular patterns.

One spring day many years ago, Francis Francis and George Selwyn Marryat were fishing the Old Barge at Winchester There was the usual parade of rods waving backwards and forwards, the wielders of them being spaced perhaps ten yards apart. Marryat was as usual killing fish, and Francis on that day could not get a rise. He was separated by some three or four other fishermen from Marryat, and presently asked his neighbour to pass the word up to Marryat that "Francis would like to know what fly he was killing with."

This message duly reached Marryat, who, after asking to have the question repeated, promptly replied, "The driver." "The driver" was duly passed down to Francis as the answer, and naturally, not liking to admit that he did not know such a pattern, he merely said, "Thank Marryat for me," and, so as to look as if the information was of use, presently changed his fly. He still could not get a rise, and did not kill a trout all day, while Marryat had a nice basket of two or three brace.

After dinner Francis remarked to Marryat. "What on earth did that silly message about the fly mean?" Said Marryat: "I was told that Francis wanted the name of the fly I was killing with, and I replied 'the driver.'" "Yes," remarked Francis, "that was the message I received; but what fly is it? I do not know such a pattern." "You silly old chump!" said Marryat, "can't you see? Not the fly, but the driver"

I fear that I should not be doing justice to the memory of one of the best friends I ever had unless I added a few words here. Marryat was full of wit and repartee, and his conversation abounded in *bons mots*, but he would have been the last to wish this little joke to be taken *au grand sérieux*. He was always trying new materials and new methods to make the artificial fly a better imitation of the natural insect, and had he been spared to this day there is no doubt in my mind that he would have warmly approved the new patterns, and very possibly would himself have abjured the use of any others

As all readers of Francis's works must have realised, he too was fully persuaded of the importance of matching in the artificial the colour of the natural insect, as tending to remove one of the causes of suspicion in a well-educated trout, and thus inducing it to fasten, instead of merely *coming short* to the angler's flies.

CHAPTER IV

OLIVE, PALE WATERY, AND IRON-BLUE SPINNERS

THE spinners of the smaller Ephemeridæ in their dressing present, in my opinion, the greatest novelty and the greatest improvement effected in the new series of patterns. The use of hackle points for the wings is not a novel departure, nor is the placing of the hackle-point wings in a horizontal position altogether an innovation. For many years the best patterns of spent gnats have been dressed with four hackle points in this horizontal position, representing the wings, and it was Williamson's idea to use two hackles in a similar position for the wings of all these flimsy insects which are so much lighter and more delicate than the imagines of the *Ephemeræ*.

When thus dressed the females are intended to represent the imagines ovipositing or when spent—*i.e* when they have voided all their eggs. The males thus dressed show accurately the attitude on the water of the male imagines at the final stage, when, having completed their share of the work of procreation, they fall almost lifeless on the surface and float down with the stream. Both sexes under these conditions serve as food for the fish, but as practically all the females fall on the water, while a large proportion of the males die on the land, the former are far more often present, and therefore are far more likely to tempt the fish.

The dressing of the male spinners referred to in this chapter is a great stride in advance of anything of a similar nature done before in respect to the bodies. The bodies of the imagines of the males in these species are almost transparent, and nothing has, to my mind, imitated the appearance of this part of them so well as the horsehair, dyed or white, worked on the bare hook which is used in the present series. I first saw it in some patterns of pale watery duns dressed a few years since, and realising its good features, adopted it at once for these flies.

In reference to the use of these patterns, it is almost necessary to recapitulate briefly some of the facts connected with the metamorphosis of the Ephemeridæ. The eggs as deposited by the imago in the water hatch out in the form of an active nymph, which, as it grows, sheds its skin from time to time. When approaching the first change it develops—one on each side of the thorax—two elongated, somewhat pear-shaped, dark-coloured sacs, in which the wings of the insect are packed in a manner somewhat resembling the folding of an umbrella.

The nymph, when ready to effect the change to the subimago or the first winged stage, swims up to the surface of the water, and when it arrives there the entire body is inflated and distended, until at length the integument splits along the back of the thorax. The subimago first pushes its thorax through the slit in the outer skin, and then the head emerges, and as a rule it then struggles until it has disengaged its six legs; next the wings, one at a time, emerge from the shuck, and the fly draws up its abdomen until it has extricated its body and setæ clear of the envelope. It often rests on the floating shuck until the wings are sufficiently dried and hardened by the air to be able to support the insect in a short flight.

If it is not annexed by fish or bird, it makes the best of its way ashore, and pitches on a bough, or a sedge or reed, and remains there—preferably on the shady side if it is sunny, and on the leeward side if it is windy—until the time arrives for the next metamorphosis. It may here be noted that the time which elapses between the emergence of the subimago from the nymphal shuck and the assumption of the imago form is entirely dependent on the temperature, being accelerated by heat and retarded by cold.

When the metamorphosis takes place the subimago splits open at the back of the front section of the thorax, and leaving a perfect skin of the head, legs, thorax, wings, abdomen, and setæ, the imago or perfect and mature insect emerges. If a male, it joins the swarms of other members of the same sex of the same species which are dancing in the air, and if it is a female, when it leaves the shelter of the bough or sedge on which it was poised, the act of coition takes place.

Soon after this the female returns to the water to lay its eggs. This is accomplished in one of three ways. Some individuals will be seen hovering over the water, dipping down and just touching the surface with the tail end of their bodies. This action will wash off a few of the eggs, which sink rapidly to the bottom of the river, and the operation is repeated until all the eggs have been deposited. Other individuals of the same species will set their wings back, bring them together at the tips so as to enclose a minute air-bubble, and crawl down a post, or a blade of grass or reed, into the water, and deposit their eggs at the spot they have selected as most suitable for their reception.

The sherry spinner, or imago of *Ephemerella ignita*, carries a bunch of blue-green eggs against the penultimate segment of its abdomen in a round ball, and these are dropped *en masse*, sink to the bottom, and are there hatched. The eggs are enveloped in a kind of sac of gelatinous matter, and the egg mass swells very much in the water.

All spinners, whether males or females, after their life's work of procreation is completed, fall almost lifeless, the females generally on the stream, and the males sometimes on the land and sometimes on the water.

It is consequently evident that the females are on the water twice during their brief life in the imago state, once when ovipositing and once when all the eggs have been voided. The male, on the other

hand, is only on the water *occasionally*, at the very last
stage of all, when it is spent. I say occasionally,
because a very considerable proportion of the males
fall on the land. It should also be remembered that
the males are polygamous, so that in their case the
last stage of existence is prolonged by nature until
all the females of the same brood have laid their
eggs.

The females select comparatively calm and mild
weather for the work of oviposition, so that they may
be expected to be busily engaged in this work on a
still morning or afternoon in April, and in mornings,
afternoons, and evenings of the other spring and the
summer months. In hot weather the majority of the
female spinners will be seen ovipositing in the early
evening, provided it is calm and not too cold. The
damp, misty exhalation which often hangs over the
surface of the water in the evening, after a very hot
day, as a white mist—generally called a *tablecloth* by
dry-fly men—often seems to make them postpone
this work to a more favourable season. Hence the
general ill success of the angler on evenings when this
tablecloth rises at or about sunset.

The reader can infer from this brief life-history
that the male spinners are not nearly such important
patterns for the dry-fly fisherman as the females ; but
there are days when individual fish will rise to the
males and not look at the females. Thus if the duns
out during the days have been, say, olives and iron-
blues, and fish taking spinners can be tempted by

the females of neither of these two species, it is always well to try the males.

Trout or grayling taking the natural spinners generally rise very quietly, and the flies themselves, lying as they do on the surface with their wings extended flat on the water, are almost invisible to the naked eye. For many years it was the custom of all of us to jump at the conclusion that fish rising to invisible insects on the surface of the stream, especially during the day, were taking one of the many forms of small Diptera generally designated as *smuts*. Williamson was the first to cast doubts on this supposition, and he was inclined to advance the theory that the chalkstream trout did not feed on smuts at all. Modern writers on the subject have not, from their observations, been able to accept his theory in its entirety, but are generally agreed that a very large proportion of what we used to call *smutting* fish are, in fact, taking the spent imagines of the smaller Ephemeridæ.

One day in June 1904 I was fishing a friend's water on the Itchen, the other rods being my host, hostess, and a doctor friend, all good fishers. It was a dull day with north-easterly wind and occasional showers, and during the morning we all found the fish what an old keeper I knew used to call " werry careful," so that, beyond returning a few fish under the pound limit, we did nothing. After a refreshing tea in the fishing hut we separated to try and fish seriously, and I went up some little distance so as to leave the stretch nearest to the hut for the lady

The yellow may dun (*Heptagenia sulphurea*) was hatching out freely, and occasional rises could be seen. My host was of opinion that the trout were taking the yellow may dun, and tried all the best imitations he could find of this very elegant and prettily coloured insect. Personally, I am not a believer in the efficacy of this fly, as in the many hundreds of autopsies I have made I have only found one specimen among the heterogeneous collection of insects, crustaceans, molluscs, &c., in the stomachs of the trout. I may here remark, too, that in all my autopsies I have only once found a turkey brown (*Leptophlebia submarginata*) in a Test or Itchen fish.

I could see a few olive spinners dipping and dropping their eggs, so put up one of the female olive spinners. After a long walk I came to a point where the fish were apparently taking fairly well, but it was very difficult fishing, owing to trees, boughs, and heavy sedge-beds, and the trout were preternaturally on the alert, so that stalking them was far from an easy matter. Occasionally, however, I could get a rise, and in the end, by a little after seven o'clock, I had killed two brace of pretty fish weighing 4 lbs. 11 oz. —a very even lot. Each of the other rods got a single fish, and of these one was killed with a red quill, and a second, I think, with the female olive spinner.

Two days later, on the St. Cross water, I had very similar experience on a very similar day. During the morning I returned five (one of which was just sizable), and lost a fair fish of about $1\frac{1}{2}$ lbs., with

K

male and female pale watery duns, and in the after-noon with the female olive spinner killed three fish weighing in the aggregate 4 lbs. Williamson was very fond of this pattern, and in a good-tempered sort of chaffing spirit called it my " female triumph "

To go back to the Test, let me recall a fine day in May with slight and variable breezes—my diary note as to the weather reads thus: "Wind light southerly, then south-easterly, then easterly, then north-easterly, and finally westerly. Thunder-clouds about, and quite mild." As to the insects visible on the water my notes read. "A fair show of black gnats, a few duns—olive, iron-blue, and pale watery —and a good number of mayflies, not taken."

I was on the main river, and found a fish rising in a desultory sort of manner. I tried olives, iron-blues, and pale watery duns of both sexes. I tried black gnats, welshman's button, and even as a last resource mayflies, but could not meet with the smallest appearance of response. Of course, as I only cast two or three times with any one pattern, and gave the fish long rests between whiles and when changing the fly, it was not surprising to find that the entire morning was consumed over this fish.

After lunch a female olive spinner was knotted on, as there were a few imagines ovipositing; but the fish was as indifferent to this as to all the other patterns tried in vain over it. When one is non-plussed in this way, it is always well to devote some time to study of the surface of the water, if only to

gain an idea of another pattern to try. In this
instance I caught from the river a spent female olive
spinner, so put up the olive (red) spinner female.
At the first cast the fish turned at the fly, followed
it a few feet downstream, took it, and after a very
stubborn resistance was landed, a good male trout of
2 lbs. 10 oz.

Walking upstream some two hundred yards, I
caught sight of another rising fish immediately under
my own bank. Getting into position and working
out the requisite length of line, I put the same fly to
the trout, feeling full of confidence in the prospect of
its success. It came over the fish to an inch, and
after floating well down below it was returned, dried
thoroughly, and after a few minutes' rest put again in
the right place. The idea with which my mind was
for the moment possessed, that I had discovered the
medicine of the moment, was, as so often happens,
rudely dispelled.

I could see nothing on the water when the fish
rose, and so tried the male black gnat, and then the
female, but to neither of these tempting morsels did
the trout make the smallest movement, although from
time to time it would slowly and gently put its nose
to the surface and suck in some floating insect. I
then changed my fly to the olive spinner female, the
imitation of the ovipositing imago of the female
olive. At the first correct cast the fish came very
slowly, fastened, and was after a time killed, a female
of 2 lbs. 1 oz.

On my way back to the fishing hut I picked up one more with the same pattern, a female of 1 lb. 6 oz.; but as that season we did not kill female fish under 2 lbs. or males under 1½ lbs. it was duly and safely returned to its native element

The olive (red) spinner female is a most useful fly, and should be tried on all occasions when the fisherman finds himself in a difficulty with a trout rising fitfully. It should, I think, be considered as the modern improved substitute for the old standard red quill

A reference to the diary shows that on the Itchen on the 13th and 14th September 1904 I had sport with it under such varying conditions as to merit some details. The 13th was a fine close day with light south-west wind, and the fish were not only very shy, but when they did rise, came so short that one could not hook them. About 6 p.m., although no fly could be seen on the surface, there were a few fish rising, and of course, as usual in the Itchen, the water was gin clear After trying various female and male spinners I put up this pattern and killed a brace of trout, 2 lbs. 7 oz.

The next day, the 14th, was rough with strong southerly winds and heavy rain, during which two undersized fish were returned. About three o'clock the water got as thick as peasoup, and while it was in this condition I tried a variety of flies over casual feeding fish. With the olive (red) spinner female I killed three of 3 lbs. 8 oz, but could not get a rise to any

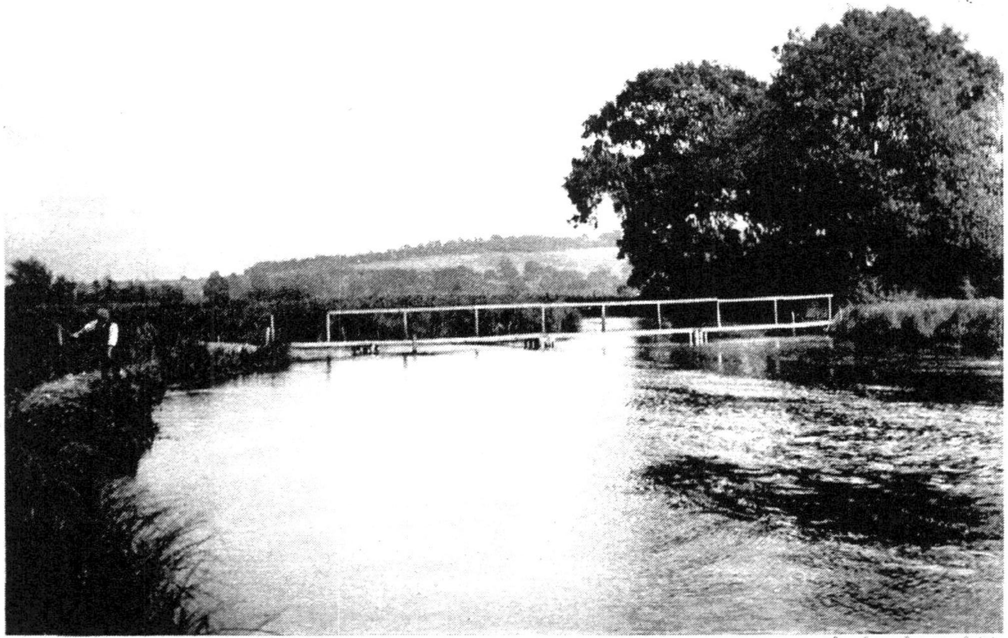

PLATE XXXIV

Swan Electric Engraving Co. Ltd.

The Upper Boundary.

other pattern. Soon after four o'clock the water cleared,
and although I could rise a great number and prick
a few of the feeding trout, not one would fasten.

From experiences on the Test I could multiply
instances when the only fly with which I could tempt
a rising fish was this same spent female olive with
the *dead leaf* coloured body. In the spot depicted
in Plate XXXIV. I can remember catching four
fish with this pattern on one occasion.

The pale watery spinners, like the duns of the
same species, are not, according to my personal experience, very killing patterns on the Test, but on their
days they are most useful on the Itchen. Thus I
find that in the latter stream on the 16th September
1904, a fresh fine day with light south-east wind, the
pale watery spinner female picked up five well-conditioned trout, aggregating 5 lbs. 6 oz. in weight,
before 1 P.M.; and for the rest of the day, beyond
losing two and pricking a few other fish, I only
killed one more of 1 lb. 2 oz. with the small dark
sedge.

The iron-blue spinner female is a good pattern to
try during the late spring and summer months, more
especially in the heat of the day. I would advise the
angler to disregard entirely the beaten-up keepers and
others that during the heat of the day it is *impossible*
to find rising trout, and it is an endeavour to catch
them. The word *impossible* in this sense should be
for ever banished from the dictionary of the sportsman. It may be difficult to accomplish, and one may

other pattern. Soon after four o'clock the water cleared, and although I could rise a great number and prick a few of the feeding trout, not one would fasten

From experiences on the Test I could multiply instances when the only fly with which I could tempt a rising fish was this same spent female olive with the *dead leaf* coloured body. In the spot depicted in Plate XXXIV. I can remember catching four fish with this pattern on one occasion.

The pale watery spinners, like the duns of the same species, are not, according to my personal experience, very killing patterns on the Test, but on their days they are most useful on the Itchen. Thus I find that in the latter stream on the 16th September 1904, a fresh fine day with light south-east wind, the pale watery spinner female picked up five well-conditioned trout, aggregating 5 lbs. 6 oz. in weight, before 1 P M , and for the rest of the day, beyond losing two and pricking a few other fish, I only killed one more of 1 lb. 2 oz with the small dark sedge.

The iron-blue spinner female is a good pattern to try during the late spring and summer months, more especially in the heat of the day. I would advise the angler to disregard entirely the dicta of keepers and others that during the heat of the day it is *impossible* to find rising trout, and if found, *impossible* to catch them. The word *impossible* is one which should be for ever banished from the dictionary of the sportsman. It may be difficult to accomplish, and one may often fail, but *Perseverantia omnia vincit*, and the dry-fly man must have patience and persevere even under the most adverse conditions if he wishes to extract the maximum of satisfaction from the pursuit of his sport.

On a hot day he should start at a reasonable hour, after a substantial breakfast, and leisurely make his way to the river-side; let him put up his rod, thoroughly fat the reel line to make it float, and after attaching a four-yard cast, let it soak thoroughly in the river for a full half-hour. No abnormally fine-drawn gut is required, but an ordinary cast, quite stout at the upper end and gradually tapering to what is called the finest natural gut at the point, should be used. I have qualified the description of the fine gut as natural by the addition of the words "so called," because I am told on the very best authority that the gut sold under this appellation is as a rule slightly drawn through the steel plates. The late John Hammond of Winchester used to describe it as "*just regulated*," which in his quaint parlance no doubt meant drawn sufficiently to make it of uniform thickness throughout its length.

Above all, there need be no hurry, the fisherman, encumbered by his waders and multifarious paraphernalia, will be hot enough without this, and he has many hours of daylight before him during which he may well find trout rising, to all of which he may with care present a fly with fair hopes of success. He should dress as lightly as he dares; but I fear that

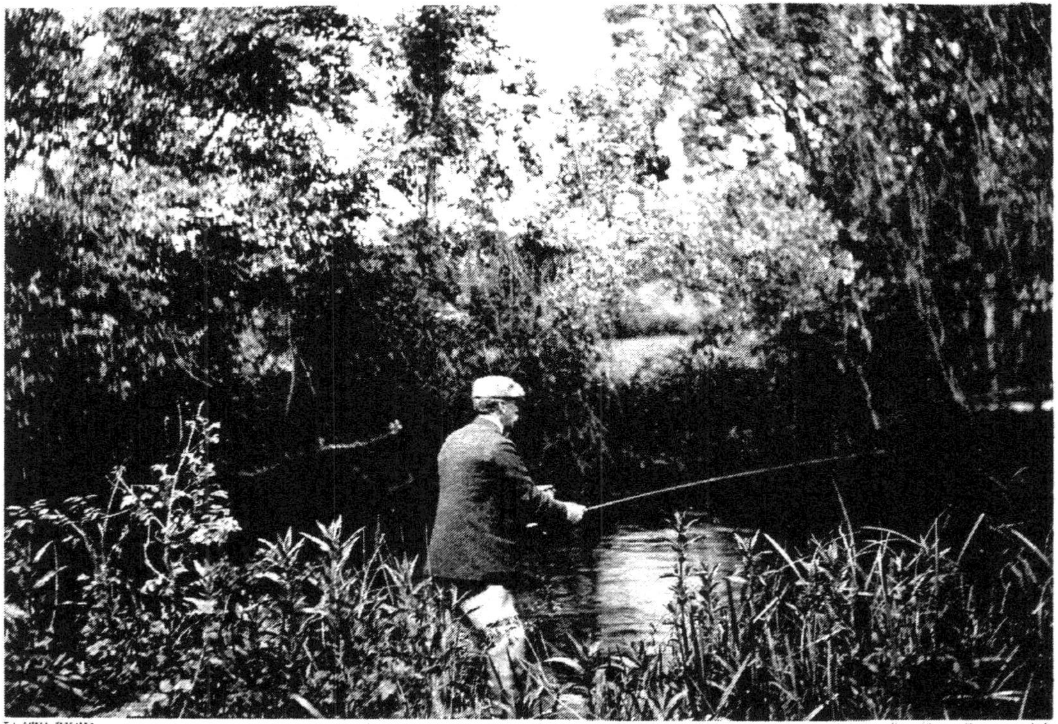

PLATE XXXV

Swan Electric Engraving Co. Ltd

An Ideal Spot for a Hot Day.

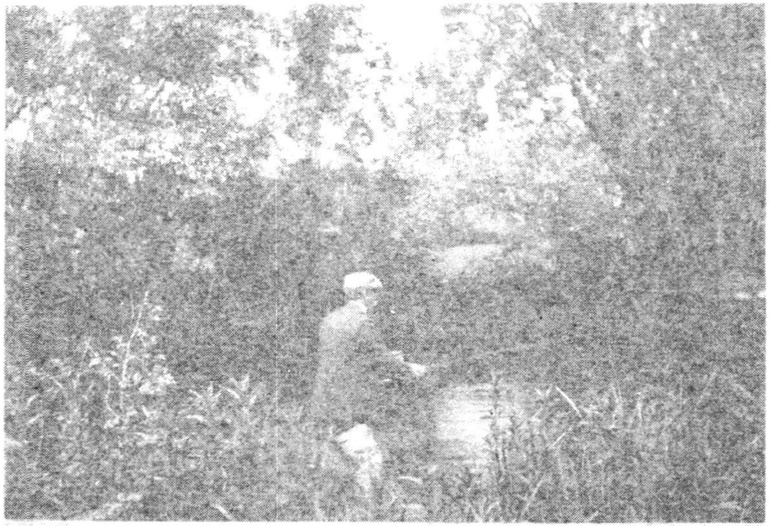

A Brook Trout Stream, Pike Bay

waders are an absolute necessity, unless he cares to brave the twinges of gout and rheumatism in later middle life or old age, consequent on wet feet and damp knees.

A short study of the placid stream with the field-glass will soon tell him all he wants to know about the species of the few flies on the water. Further scrutiny, this time preferably without the field-glass, may well show him a trout a few inches under water, moving from side to side, probably in the immediate vicinity of a heavy weed-patch, coming slowly to the surface, examining and taking at longish intervals one or more of the various insects floating down to it. The fish itself and every movement will be visible in the bright sunlight, and it is scarcely needful to warn the experienced hand that he must lie low, keep out of the range of the trout's vision, and fish with the horizontal cast. I know no more ideal place for a hot day than that shown in Plate XXXV.

For patterns of flies, the two sexes of black gnat, the brown ant, and the female spinners of the olive, pale watery, or iron-blue, or occasionally a sedge, will be sufficient variety. He must watch the position of the trout at the moment of casting, and place the artificial, say, twelve inches above it, of course taking every precaution to avoid drag and to combine delicacy and accuracy in the first cast. A change of fly is often efficacious; not that it is suggested that a trout taken in this manner is generally dainty in its choice of food, but because the tendency of all and every one of us is to throw too often, and this fault is to some degree remedied by the period of rest enforced during the operation of removing one and substituting another pattern.

A large proportion of the feeding fish may, it is true, come short, and some of those that fasten may well succeed in getting away either at the first plunge or later, even when almost within reach of the landing-net. Anglers who have not tried this hot-weather fishing will find in it many charms and many dis-appointments, but will perhaps derive some con-solation from the reflection that fishing the floating fly in brilliant sunshine over rising fish is, after all, the highest form of fly-fishing imaginable, and is the fairest trial of skill pitted against the natural shyness of the chalk-stream trout, in many instances increased by the education they have received at the hands of our brother anglers.

Every movement of the trout, the natural insects floating down to it, the artificial following the same course when deftly placed exactly on the right spot, the rise, and every detail of playing the trout when hooked, will be enacted in full view of the fisherman. Hot he will be, no doubt, and return bathed in pro-fuse perspiration from head to foot, but yet I may venture to predict that he will not suffer from the heat to the same extent as when lounging about watching cricket or lawn-tennis, or even lazing indoors.

As an example of this method of fishing I would cite my experience on the 1st June 1903, a very hot

day with light north-easterly wind. After pottering
about until lunch time, I started about 2.30 to walk
down the canal length of the St. Cross water to the
lowest beat of the fishery, where the mayfly was
plentiful and the artificial generally proved successful
in killing some good fish On my way down a
fish rising slowly in a somewhat interesting place
attracted my attention

A heavy mass of cut weeds was kept jammed by
the current against a weed rack above a wide carrier
which at the time was empty. The trout was rising
in the dead water immediately above the lodged weeds,
and, as might be expected in such a position, moved
about considerably.

The wind was downstream and towards the bank
from which I was fishing, and the shape of the weed
mass and a bend in the bank of the river made it
necessary to be rather close to the fish. As all my
readers know, it is a great disadvantage when casting
against the wind to be obliged to locate oneself too
near to the fish, because the shorter the length of line
the more difficult it is to place the fly accurately into
the wind. Another difficulty in this position was that
the line had to be laid on the weeds, and it was
necessary to recover the fly very smoothly and without
jerk so as to avoid getting hung up Should that
happen, any movement of the weed mass itself caused
by trying to disengage the fly would almost certainly
scare the fish and put it off the rise.

Selecting a well-dressed iron-blue spinner female,

I tied it on to the gut, and having judged the length of line required I waited for a favourable moment to cast A lull in the wind and a momentary obscuration of the sun gave me the opportunity, and the fly was despatched on its errand. It landed short, and the work of getting it clear of the weed mass without raising my head, which would have scared the fish, was at length accomplished Then a few additional feet of line enabled me to place the fly just where it was wanted

The fish rose, fought well, trying in vain to dive under the weed mass, and when foiled in this endeavour gave a grand run out into the stream and down at a great pace. After this it gave in and came to the net in rather a tame fashion. It was a large fish for this water—a male trout of 2 lbs. 6 oz.—but one which evidently had lost considerably in weight since the days of its full vigour of youth. Later in the day, when returning from the mayfly reach, my friend asked me to have a cast with a new rod he was using. With the same pattern I then killed, just below the place where the big one succumbed earlier in the day, another trout of 1 lb. 4 oz.

Another June experience on the Test was not quite so satisfactory for me I had a friend staying with me, a very good fisherman, and being anxious to find him some sport, suggested that we should separate for the morning, one going up and the other down the main Test. He went down, and as his experience exactly tallied with my own, I need only give mine. Here and there could be seen a fish bulging, but the hatch of fly was so sparse that it was barely possible to secure more than a single specimen of any species. There were certainly some smuts on the water, an odd olive, pale watery, and iron-blue dun, so I tried every one of these patterns without success. At last I put up an iron-blue spinner female and rose several fish, but every one came short and I had an absolute blank. My friend's fortune was very similar, but one of the fish rising to his iron-blue spinner female fastened, and he killed a pretty female trout of 2 lbs. 2 oz

The consideration of evening fishing with the various patterns of female spinners is postponed to a subsequent chapter entitled " Evening Fishing."

CHAPTER V

BLACK GNAT AND BROWN ANT

I⊤ is to be feared that, like most of my confrères who have broken out into print on dry-fly fishing, I have been guilty in the past of adding to the undigested mass of ill-considered matter written to prove the insuperable difficulty of rising and killing smutting fish. As I have before remarked, it is now a well-established fact that a large proportion of what we all used to declare were *smutting* trout are taking the imagines of the smaller Ephemeridæ, floating down with their wings outstretched at right angles to the line of their bodies At the same time it must be clearly understood that trout and grayling under certain conditions, and in the presence of considerable numbers of these tiny Diptera on the water, certainly do feed on them and take them freely.

In olden times we used to advise the angler to try a series of more or less fancy patterns when he found that the imitations of the fisherman's curse and black gnat were not successful in tempting the rising fish Such patterns as the two varieties of wickham, or red quill, for example, are so evidently in form akin to the Ephemeridæ that it is no longer a matter of surprise for us to find that a fish feeding freely on the spinners should occasionally make a mistake and risk its life by rising to such patterns of artificial fly. Nowadays we freely recognise that under these conditions the spinners are the best flies to use, and will generally kill fish feeding on the insects they represent

For the trout or grayling that is in reality feeding on *smuts* the new patterns of male and female black gnat are almost always successful. Of the two I personally much prefer the male, because, although dressed on the same size of hook, it is in appearance, owing to the lightness of the materials used in its manufacture, a far less solid structure than the female. There are, however, times when the female is taken better, and very possibly the individual fish may, like the rest of the animal kingdom, have a decided preference for one rather than the other.

The brown ant, the imitation of which, as fully set out in a previous chapter, was copied from a great flight of winged ants taken from the Itchen, is a fly which under ordinary conditions is taken greedily by the trout and grayling when it is present in great numbers. Until last year, 1909, I should have been almost prepared to assert as an incontrovertible fact that rising fish could not and would not refuse it when it was on the water, but in September of that year I had an experience which altered my opinion. I was out with a friend one day on the Test, and we could not find out what fly the fish were taking, or at least we could not tempt them to rise. All at once we both exclaimed as if with one voice that the brown ant was out in enormous numbers, and we felt quite certain that we should both get some sport. My friend at once put up one of this pattern, cast over the nearest feeding fish, but could not rise it. This was repeated over and over again, and as he was fishing very well indeed, I did not see any advantage in trying these fish myself. He had killed a pretty fish of 1 lb 13 oz. with male iron-blue in the morning, but all our endeavours failed to make it a brace, as neither the brown ant nor the imitation of any other insect on the water had the smallest attraction for these rising fish. I felt quite certain in my own mind that they were taking the ant, but it was one of those days when one could not account for the erratic behaviour of the Salmonidæ.

The brown ant is often as good a pattern for grayling as for trout, and my diary contains a good many records of its success. On one August day on the Test, the weather being showery, with thunder, heavy rain, and hot intervals, the only fish moving during the forenoon were grayling, and after trying in vain a number of other patterns, I killed two, weighing in the aggregate 3 lbs. 2 oz., with it; while on the 12th and 13th September in the same year, two grayling of 2 lbs. 4 oz., and 2 lbs. 2 oz., and a good trout, a female of 2 lbs. 2 oz., were added to the brown ant's list of victories.

One curious day may be taken as an example

of what I might style the "casual" utility of the brown ant. This was on the Itchen, also in September. An American sportsman who was anxious to see some dry-fly work had been introduced to me, and at the kind invitation of the lessee—to whose liberality and cordial welcome I owe many other pleasant days on the fishery—we went together to Winnall, a fine stretch of water immediately above the city of Winchester.

It was a hot morning, with a strong southerly wind, and there were very few duns or spinners to be seen. There were a few smuts of various descriptions, and although I had not positively secured a specimen, I was fairly certain that there were also some brown ants present.

In a slack place under our own bank a fish was roaming about, occasionally coming slowly to the top of the water and taking some tiny insect so gently as barely to disturb the smooth surface of the stream. The wind was almost straight into my face when I had gradually crept into position and assumed a more or less recumbent attitude. A careful study of the conditions and a fortunate lull enabled me to place the fly—a brown ant—quite accurately at the first attempt. A bold rise, a good run, and the usual resolute tactics culminated in the landing of a pretty trout of 1 lb. 14 oz.

This, however, exhausted the brown ant's killing powers, or rather the trial of them on this occasion. A short distance above, another rising fish came short to it, so I quickly changed to a female black gnat, and with this fly rose and pricked several fish, killing three weighing respectively 1 lb. 13 oz., 1 lb. 3 oz, and 2 lbs   This, to my mind, was a very fine bag for the Itchen, being four trout weighing in the aggregate 7 lbs. exactly.   As might be expected, after the successful morning the evening turned out wet and unpleasant, and as the fish did not rise we were both glad to return to our comfortable quarters and change to dry clothes.   My American friend was, above all, desirous of seeing how dry-fly fishing was worked, and elected to walk with me during the morning.   As an old wet-fly man he was already fully impressed with the importance of casting lightly and delicately, and he very quickly realised the absolute necessity of extreme accuracy in placing the fly to achieve any success. What appealed to him most forcibly, however, was the explanation of the various manœuvres required to prevent or retard drag in different places and under different conditions.   During the afternoon I persuaded him to fish, and his great difficulty was to prevent himself from raising his hand as the fly came down to him, so as to be able to strike quickly. This action naturally made the fly drag, but after a time he got over it.   It was almost a hopeless afternoon, and his only sport was a grayling of about 1¾ lbs., which he landed and, in accordance with the rules then in force on the fishery, he returned to the water.

Another remarkable Itchen bag was made, though not by me, about ten days later in that same September. In most fisheries there are places where large fish are present in considerable numbers but where they seldom rise, and the angler who chances to hit on a favourable day and a pattern to tempt them generally scores heavily. The pool made by the water being penned back by hatches in the upper gate of one of the old locks of the disused canal a short distance below Winchester was such a spot. Williamson, the lessee of the water, and two mutual friends were fishing, and I was walking, yarning, and generally loafing about with them. During the morning two pretty fish of 1 lb. 12 oz each were killed by Williamson in the lock, and after lunch I persuaded one of the visitors to try there.

Very soon after his arrival he killed a male fish of 1 lb. 11 oz., then lost another quite as large, and then landed a beautiful female trout over 3 lbs., but as it was evidently full of well-developed ova, he, like the sportsman he is, returned it for the benefit of the future of the fishery. He then, a good reward for his self-denial, killed in succession two more males of 2 lbs. 3 oz. and 2 lbs. 12 oz., the last in most perfect condition. The total, four trout weighing nearly 10 lbs.—albeit one was returned—was a notable one for the Itchen.

The manner in which they were caught deserves a few words of comment too. Some one had told him or he had read of a wonderful medicine for shy

L

trout called "'Tups' Indispensable," a fancy hackle pattern dressed with a pale-blue cock hackle and a body of some grey-coloured hair, which is supposed to be taken from some part of a ram—hence the name. A few bits of brilliant red seal fur are generally mixed up with the wool of the body. After killing the first, losing one, and then landing the 3-lb. female with it, he was vaunting the super-excellence of this pattern. I ventured to suggest that either of the new pattern black gnats or the brown ant would do quite as well, and he selected one of the male black gnats out of my box and put it up As he killed the two big male fish with this pattern, he has since then been a firm believer in that fly.

This tends to show how easily a pattern can achieve a reputation. The "Tups' Indispensable" is a pattern resembling in many ways some spinners, and no doubt in efficient hands can do and has done well. If my friend had been obstinate and had refused to try any other pattern, he would have been to the end of his life not only a firm believer in the efficacy of this fancy pattern, but very possibly would have declared that no other artificial fly known would have tempted the fish in that place and on that day, and might never have acquired his faith in the new pattern of black gnat male.

My dear friend Williamson was then starting his hatchery and ponds at St. Cross, and asked me to try and get him a few breeding fish for it, selecting especially trout of good size and of the appearance he particularly admired. I had two days on the 17th and 19th September, with an attendant carrying a large can in which to transport any fish alive to the breeding-ponds In these two days I secured six fish—five females weighing respectively 1 lb. 12 oz., 2 lbs., 2 lbs. 4 oz., 1 lb. 2 oz., and 1 lb. 8 oz., and one male of 1 lb. 4 oz.—all of the strain which my friend particularly affected for breeding purposes, and these were duly turned into one of the ponds. One of these fish was taken with an olive (red) spinner female, three with the female and one with the male black gnat, and the single male fish with the brown ant. I have called attention to the sexes of these fish as a further confirmation (if any is deemed necessary) of the fact that at the latter part of the season the great proportion of the rising fish are females.

I may also convey a word of warning to any of my readers who may be tempted to try and secure a breeding stock in this way. The superintendent of the hatchery at St. Cross and Williamson himself told me at a later date that the experiment had been most unsuccessful These fish would not take the horseflesh or other food given to them, naturally went back very much in condition from want of a sufficiency of food at this critical period, and the yield of ova was very poor indeed. I should not be surprised to hear that, if it had been possible to keep the produce of these eggs apart from the general stock of fry, the young fish themselves were not healthy and that the mortality among them had been quite abnormal.

The male black gnat has often helped my sport considerably, and it was prominent one Itchen day in the middle of June which had some curious features. It was a typical early summer day, with light northerly wind in the morning, gradually veering round until the vane pointed due south at sunset. The hatch of fly was sparse, and consisted of olive, pale watery, and iron-blue duns with their respective spinners; during the afternoon there were a few black gnats.

The first fly taken off the water in the morning was a female iron-blue spinner, that little transparent-winged spinner, with body of a dark rich maroon colour, which is so often seen on warm and comparatively calm days. Naturally one's impulse was to start with this pattern, and it was knotted on to the gut, which had of course been well soaked previously to soften it. The first rising fish came to it boldly and was netted in due course; then a number of feeding fish came short, and at length two more sizable fish succumbed to the fascination of the little spinner.

Then for a considerable time the few feeding fish could only be persuaded to rise in a half-hearted manner, and did not fasten. A number of apparently sizable fish were then seen feeding in comparatively close proximity, taking some minute object with the smallest possible disturbance of the surface, and all of them were travelling about, up, down, and across the stream. Evidently these trout were smutting, and although it has been proved that my friend Williamson's opinion that " Itchen trout seldom smut" is a sound one, yet here was an evident exception to the rule he laid down that the so-called smutting fish are generally taking spinners. Had he been spared to see this rise he would have been the first to admit the cogency of my arguments, the more so as they were borne out by the solid logic of fact.

As no pattern of spinner presented to these fish was rewarded with the faintest sign of approval, I put up a male black gnat, and in rapid succession killed five good trout, and returned two undersized ones, besides losing one or two more. To complete the history of the day, there was a small show of spinners at about six o'clock, so the fly was changed and a female olive spinner put up. After another undersized fish had been returned and a sizable one killed, it really appeared, with nearly three hours of gradually waning daylight before me, as if the day was likely to be a record one

Nine trout weighing exactly 10 lbs had been killed, several undersized ones had been returned, and several more lost; the spinners were on the water, and the trout were apparently settling down to an evening meal. A cast was made to a fish rising quietly under the bank, it took the fly deliberately, was hooked, ran across the river with a good strain on the bent rod; in a moment the fly came back and the fish was free. It was then only about seven o'clock and the sun was still high above the horizon, but for some unexplained reason the spinners disappeared and it was all over for the day. A casual observer moving along on the river-bank would have been quite sure that the majority of fishermen out on that particular day would have returned in a chastened spirit, with all the conceit knocked out of them, with empty flasks and empty baskets.

The female black gnat one morning towards the end of May enabled me to come with fair credit out of a gambling transaction. A friend who was fishing with me on the Oakley branch of the Test is a good sportsman, with a strong spirit of emulation, and from a bit of chaff on a day when we were fishing together on the Itchen we generally have a gamble of a very innocent description. We have a bet of one shilling on the largest fish, and another one of like amount on the greatest aggregate weight of sizable trout falling to our respective shares. Probably the most inveterate opponent of gambling would pardon this, and anyhow as the winner always presents the stakes to the keeper.

My friend, accompanied by the keeper, elected to work upstream, and taking the keeper's son to carry my net and all paraphernalia, I went down to the lower boundary of the water. It was a fine warm sunny day, with easterly to variable wind, and the majority of the fish were smutting, and very difficult to stalk or rise. After a few unsuccessful attempts, I caught sight of a fish taking fairly well at a place

PLATE XXXVI

On the Mickleham Terrace Walk

From a Photograph by J.G.

which could only be cast to with rather a long line unless one waded, and wading in a narrow, shallow stream is one of my pet aversions. I know from experience that persistence in it effectually ruins the water and makes the trout preternaturally shy, and even indulging in it occasionally will have a most pernicious effect on the behaviour of the fish.

I put up a female black gnat, and after a few casts which fell short of the place, at length the fly landed right and sailed down over the feeding fish. It took at once, and the moment it felt the point of the hook, started upstream at a great pace, went across, and tried to hang me up on a patch of floating weeds kept in place by a post on the opposite side of the river. In Plate XXXVI. the camera has assisted me to describe this part of the stream.

Pulling the trout away from this danger spot, I was soon on fair terms with it, and landed it, a very pretty male fish of 2 lbs. 6 oz. After this I walked downstream, and lost two with the male black gnat—one of these being a big one. I then killed another male of 1 lb. 10 oz., but then the fish seemed to have gone off the black gnat, so I changed to an olive (red) spinner female, and with it killed a female of 1 lb. 6 oz., besides returning three.

We then met and lunched, and I found that my friend had killed three fish aggregating 5 lbs. 10 oz., the best being a male of 2 lbs. 4 oz. My aggregate

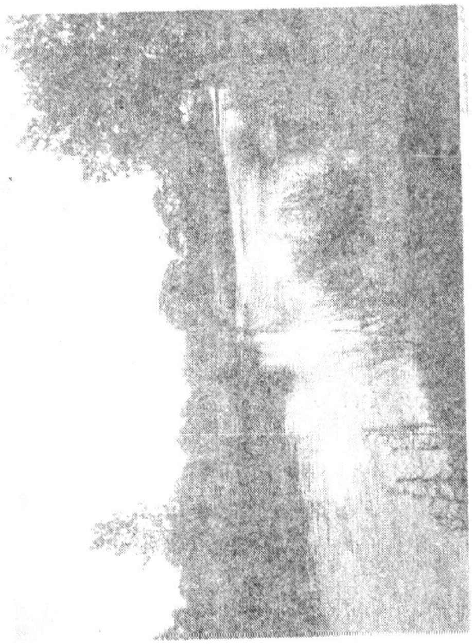

which could only be cast to with rather a long line unless one waded, and wading in a narrow, shallow stream is one of my pet aversions. I know from experience that persistence in it effectually ruins the water and makes the trout preternaturally shy, and even indulging in it occasionally will have a most pernicious effect on the behaviour of the fish.

I put up a female black gnat, and after a few casts which fell short of the place, at length the fly landed right and sailed down over the feeding fish. It took at once, and the moment it felt the point of the hook, started upstream at a great pace, went across, and tried to hang me up on a patch of floating weeds kept in place by a post on the opposite side of the river. In Plate XXXVI. the camera has assisted me to describe this part of the stream

Pulling the trout away from this danger spot, I was soon on fair terms with it, and landed it, a very pretty male fish of 2 lbs. 6 oz After this I walked downstream, and lost two with the male black gnat—one of these being a big one. I then killed another male of 1 lb. 10 oz., but then the fish seemed to have gone off the black gnat, so I changed to an olive (red) spinner female, and with it killed a female of 1 lb. 6 oz , besides returning three.

We then met and lunched, and I found that my friend had killed three fish aggregating 5 lbs. 10 oz., the best being a male of 2 lbs. 4 oz. My aggregate being three of 5 lbs. 6 oz., and my largest 2 lbs. 6 oz., the match was thus, according to golfing parlance, *halved*. The total bag of six trout, weighing 11 lbs., was to my mind a respectable one, even for two rods, during the forenoon only of what was far from a favourable day.

CHAPTER VI

THE WELSHMAN'S BUTTON

MANY years ago the discovery was made that when
the chalk-stream trout had not come on to the mayfly
although it was well up, they would often rise with
the utmost confidence to imitations of the welshman's button. The old pattern, dressed with bronze
peacock herl body, ginger or red hackle, and wings
of peacock underwing or partridge tail, was a very
poor imitation of the natural insect. Yet it must be
admitted that it often scored heavily, and the anglers
who affected the pattern often *wiped the eyes* of the
mayfly purists. Marryat and many other friends
used to chaff me unmercifully on my seeming incon-
stancy in abandoning the green drake and adopting
in its place the sober-looking welshman's button; but
many of them were inclined to follow my example
when they found that the resulting sport was so good.

None of the work of matching the colours and
selecting materials for the new patterns gave me more
pleasure than that of dealing with this species of the
family of the Sericostomatidæ. The very first year
after it had been worked out, 1904, I had an opportunity of giving it a good trial on the Itchen on the
31st May, when, with a fair hatch of mayfly which

the fish were not taking, there was also a good show of the welshman's button. With the new pattern of the male I killed three brace in succession, weighing in the aggregate 7 lbs. 9 oz., returning four, and losing several others.

The Test in 1905 afforded, as far as my own experience was concerned, a striking example of the gradual decline of mayfly fishing which since that year has been continuous The first stragglers of the mayfly showed up, as usual, about the middle of May on the lower length of the river, but there was no real rise of the fly before the 24th, and the trout then took no notice of it For the next four days the fish were left alone, so as to give them every opportunity of becoming accustomed to the appearance of *Ephemera danica* and appreciating its flavour.

On the 29th, a very hot day with southerly wind, I spent the morning full of hope, but up to two o'clock nothing appeared on the water except olive and iron-blue duns, which were apparently unnoticed by the fish. The water was very low, in consequence of some of the farmers above having just turned the bulk of the water into their water meadows. At last a fair show of mayfly came up, and the fish started rushing about, fighting, occasionally making loud *floops*, and generally creating a commotion in the river.

Some of the old school of fly fishermen call this taking the mayfly, and are very wroth at being contradicted on this point They say that the fish are "running after the fly," and as a corroboration of their theory advance the argument that the trout under these conditions will occasionally rise to the artificial mayfly. Cross-examination will generally elicit from them the admission that a very small proportion of them are hooked, and of those hooked all but an occasional unfortunate victim get away. When told that this rising, pricking, hooking, and losing of large numbers of the biggest trout only result in their becoming abnormally shy, and even tend to drive them off the mayfly altogether, our friends are as a rule simply incredulous, or perhaps impute the advice to interested motives.

Trout taking the winged subimago of the mayfly neither rush, fight, floop, nor splash, and certainly do not run after it. This extreme activity is displayed in attempting to catch the lively nymphs rising through the water, on the surface of which the winged sub-imago emerges from its nymphal envelope. If the fly emerges just at the moment the fish reaches it, either the fly or the shuck is taken, and the loud floop or splash is made when the trout seizes and devours the nymph in mid-water. On the day in question all these symptoms were fully in evidence, and to aggravate the difficulties further, the low state of the water made the trout preternaturally shy of the fly, gut, or any appearance of drag.

There were a considerable number of imagines of the welshman's button on the water, and the pattern of the male, which is smaller than the female and appreciably darker in colouration, is generally more successful in my hands than the female. I make this statement with some mental reservation, because I am always prone to select the smaller of two likely patterns, and in this particular fly the sexes are very dissimilar in size. Given a preference on the angler's part for a particular pattern, it is fair to predict that he will use it more often and be more successful with it than with any other.

To achieve success with this fly it is essential to practise a certain degree of self-denial, and one must determine to fish with the head quite as much as with the hands. If one is desirous of obtaining good sport without pricking, losing, and scaring an inordinate proportion of the feeding trout, the golden rule must be observed of selecting with the utmost care the most likely fish and refraining from casting to any other. The splashing rise or noisy floop is not made on the surface, and, other things being equal, the fish taking in shallow water are probably feeding on welshman's button, and are therefore far more likely to be tempted than those following the mayfly nymphs up from a considerable depth

If possible, place your fly, thoroughly dry and well cocked, a foot in front of the trout's nose at the moment it is close to the surface; and, above all, remember that the first cast is in every case the most likely one to tempt the feeding fish, and take the greatest care that it is made with *accuracy and delicacy combined.* If it is taken, strike as deliberately as possible—in fact, it is barely possible to be too late in striking. If the fly is not taken at the first cast, wait patiently, and let the fish get the full flavour of a few more specimens of the natural insect, either the pupæ rising through the water or the winged imagines on the surface, before making a second cast.

If a fish rises to your fly and does not drown it, do not strike, and do not cast to it again. This is technically called *refusing a fly*, a form of coming short, and remember that it is not once in a hundred times that a trout misses the fly, either natural or artificial The cause of the trout refusing or coming short is invariably either that they are not keen on the particular insect, possibly because they are not taking surface food at all, or that something has occurred to rouse their suspicions and engender caution at the last moment.

Following these rules, I landed five trout and one grayling in less than two hours on the day described, returning the grayling and two of the trout as under the 2-lb. limit, and killing three perfectly conditioned fish of 2 lbs. 7 oz., 2 lbs. 3 oz., and 2 lbs. 1 oz. On the 31st May I killed another trout of 2 lbs. 14 oz., and on the 1st June two more of 2 lbs. 7 oz. and 2 lbs. 5 oz.

In the *Field* of June 27, 1908, an article appeared from my pen, "Mayflies and Welshman's Button," which is so appropriate that I propose quoting it almost *in extenso.* Here, too, let me express my thanks to the proprietors of that, the first sporting paper in the world, for their kind permission to give in book form any of the articles I have written for them

"Another early June has waned, and it must be recorded that the mayfly has again been conspicuous, if not by its absence, at least by its rarity on the Test Some of the fishermen view with feelings of grief its gradual decrease in numbers, and others are content to anticipate with comparative equanimity its probable total disappearance from the list of their killing flies.

" In olden times the mayfly week or fortnight was *the* debauch during the season of many hard-working votaries of the dry fly, and the feature most strongly impressed on their memories has been that, on the few days when the fish were taking, those killed were exceptionally large even for this, the premier chalk stream of 'Merrie England.' It may perhaps be a consolation to some of them to know that a fly which has always been present, and has often been a good killer during the drake season, has certainly increased of late years, and may prove in some degree a substitute for *Ephemera danica.*

" When the late Mr. Marryat and I first devoted ourselves to the study of the insects on which the chalk-stream trout fed, we were most anxious that the scientific naming of them should be beyond question. Specimens for identification were submitted to one or more of the leading authorities of the day, and in the case of the welshman's button they were sent to the late Mr. M'Lachlan, whose 'Monograph of the Trichoptera' is the standard

work on the subject to-day, and to the Rev. A. E.
Eaton, one of the most eminent living entomologists.
Without hesitation it was named by both of them
as *Sericostoma personatum*, one of the Sericostomatidæ, a group of the large family of Trichoptera
or caddis-flies. (Any one wishing to study the life-
history of this caddis-fly will find in the cabinet of
natural insects at the Fly Fishers' Club a series of
mounts showing its gradual development from the
egg to the imago)

"When working out the new set of patterns,
a considerable time was devoted to this particular
insect, and the imitations of both sexes are generally
deemed to be fairly true to nature, and are certainly
good killers. The female, which is—as usual among
the Trichoptera [1]—considerably the larger, has wings
of a lighter hue than her smaller and darker-
winged mate. When on the water it is often mis-
taken for the alder (*Sialis lutaria*), even by the best
judges, but once the insect is caught there can be no
doubt as to its identity.

"It may be remembered, too, that the welshman's
button pupates in the water in its stony case, the
pupa tearing its way out of the case, rising to the
surface, and there splitting open the thin skin in which
it is enveloped. The imago emerges, and later the
female imago lays its eggs in or on the water, so that
it is on the water at two stages of its existence.

"The alder larva, when fully grown, crawls ashore,
pupates in the ground, and the imago or perfect
insect emerges. The female lays its eggs on sedges

---

[1] Exceptions to this rule are found in the sexes of many of the
Leptoceridæ, and one or two isolated species of other families

at the margin of the stream, and the larvæ, when hatched, crawl down into the mud at the bottom of the river and there pass their larval stage. Thus the alder has at no part of its existence as a winged insect any necessity to be on the water, and it is only there when a sudden gust of wind blows it on to the surface or when some other unforeseen occurrence precipitates it on to the water

"On May 28th in this year the first mayflies commenced hatching out. The expression 'hatching' is used generally by fly fishermen, not in its scientific sense as meaning hatching from the egg, but to express the metamorphosis from the nymph to sub-imago or imago, whichever is the first winged stage. As they were rather numerous, many of us were imprudently predicting an old-fashioned rise of the drake, to be followed by an exciting period of fishing with the spent gnat, as the imago after completed reproduction is usually, but incorrectly, named by anglers.

"Simultaneously the welshman's button appeared, and continued in considerable numbers until past the middle of the month of June. On the 29th May the mayflies were more numerous, but the fish did not rise at them, and from this time a few were seen daily until June 11th, but they were never appreciated by the trout.

"On the 29th it blew half a gale from the northeast, and the male welshman's button being used, one trout of 1 lb. 11 oz was killed in the water under my observation With the same fly on the 30th, a close thundery day with easterly wind, four trout, 1 lb 4 oz., 2 lbs. 8 oz., 1 lb. 10 oz, and 1 lb. 6 oz., were taken,

and on June 2nd two more of 1 lb. 6 oz. and 2 lbs.,
while on the 5th three of 1 lb. 15 oz., 1 lb. 7 oz., and
1 lb. 11 oz., also fell victims to the seductive male
welshman's button.   On all these days a considerable number of trout below the limit of the water,
1¼ lb., were returned.   These figures are given as
showing the sport during what was considered in
olden times the cream of the mayfly rise."

The year 1909 was again a disappointing one for
the lover of the mayfly, as the fly was scarce and the
trout did not take the few that appeared with any
great avidity.   On the 29th May I killed a brace,
2 lbs. 11 oz. and 1 lb. 8 oz., with the male welshman's
button, and on the next day a friend killed one of
1 lb. 8 oz., and two grayling of 1 lb. 8 oz. and 2 lbs.,
on the same pattern.   Finding that after this the fish
did not come well to his fly, he changed to the female,
and killed in succession three more trout, 1 lb. 4 oz.,
2 lbs, and 1 lb. 4 oz, and a grayling of 1 lb. 4 oz.,
with it.   On the 31st my friend killed two trout of 1 lb.
4 oz. and 1 lb. 6 oz, and three grayling of 1 lb., 1 lb., and
1 lb. 8 oz., with the male, while I secured three trout
of 1 lb 8 oz., 1 lb. 8 oz., and 1 lb. 12 oz with the male,
and two with the female of 2 lbs. 1 oz. and 2 lbs.

The 2nd June, three trout of 1 lb. 8 oz, 1 lb.
6 oz, and 1 lb. 10 oz., on the 3rd two of 1 lb. 4 oz.
and 1 lb. 6 oz, on the 4th a single one of 1 lb. 10 oz.,
and on the 5th five of 1 lb. 4 oz., 1 lb. 6 oz., 2 lbs.
2 oz., 1 lb. 7 oz., and 1 lb. 7 oz., and three grayling of
1 lb. 11 oz., 2 lbs 2 oz, and 2 lbs. 13 oz., and on the

7th three of 1 lb. 4 oz., 2 lbs. 5 oz , and 1 lb. 10 oz., constituted the joint bag of my friend and myself with the male welshman's button. I was on a friend's water on the 8th, and hooked a huge fish on the male welshman's button, which broke me ignominiously in heavy weeds, and I killed one of 1 lb. 8 oz.

The 9th June was a moderately fine day, with northerly wind, and, accompanied by a friend, I wandered over to the main river—my guest electing to work down to the lower end of the beat, while I remained at about the centre of the water on which the right of fishing is in my hands. I saw a fish rise just behind a boat moored to our bank, tried it with an iron-blue dun male, and with olives, also with the female spinners of both these species.

After a time a welshman's button came down fluttering on the surface, in the way so typical of this insect, and the rising fish went out some yards to secure it. At once the male button was put up, and landed right at the first attempt. The trout rose, and the moment it was hooked ran upstream, then turned and tried to get under the boat, but being foiled in this, came downstream at a good pace, and in a few minutes was in the net, a beautiful male of 1 lb. 8 oz.

Just above Oakley Hole there is a ford which in former days was the road across the river; very possibly there is still a right of way there, but as it has not been used for years, the further end of it

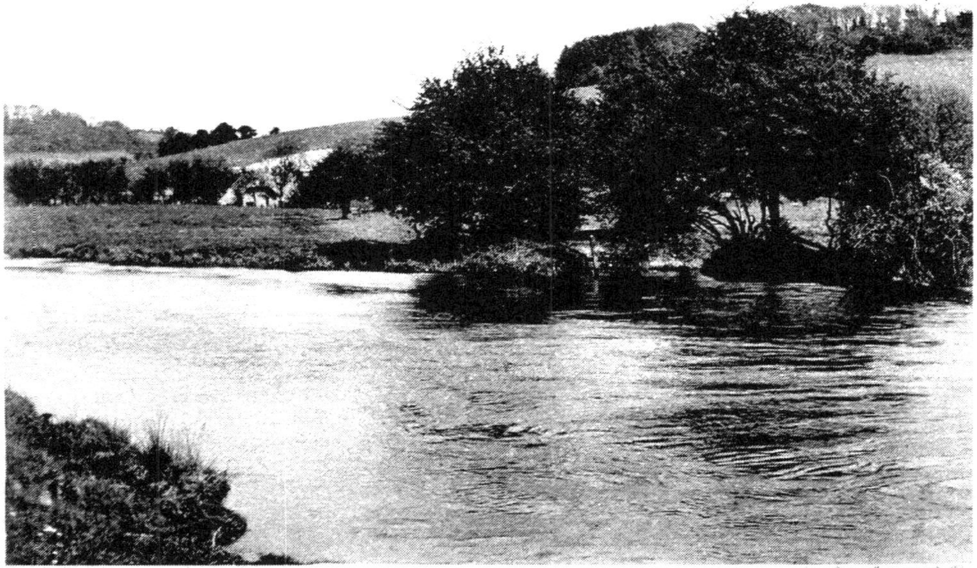

PLATE XXXVII

The Ford above Oakley Hole

Swan Electric Engraving Co.

under the eastern bank has been stopped by a series
of posts and rails. A short distance below these
posts and rails there is a rough run close to the
opposite bank, and the general appearance of this
part of the Test is fairly portrayed in Plate XXXVII.

Just below this rough run a good fish was feeding
and splashing about, and as the distance was quite
twenty-five yards, I wondered if I could put a fly over
it with the wind blowing downstream and towards
my bank. After a few attempts the cast came off, and
the fish came at the fly with a rush, and when hooked
started downstream under the opposite bank at a
great pace.

Having to clamber over a rough kind of fence to
follow it on my bank, I slacked at once, handed the
rod to the keeper until I was over the fence, and then
took the rod from his hands. When a fish feels the
line slack it generally sinks down in the water and
remains fairly quiescent, and this one was no exception to the rule. The moment I tightened on it,
another rush—this time upstream—made my reel
sing until I feared that I should have to clamber
back over the fence for fear of having all my line
run out.

At length it turned and again tore downstream,
all the time being almost under the far bank.
Gradually I got on terms with it, and in a few minutes
we could see a large fish fighting deep down in Oakley
Hole. Naturally it tried its level best to hang me
up in every weed-bed, but the continual strain at last

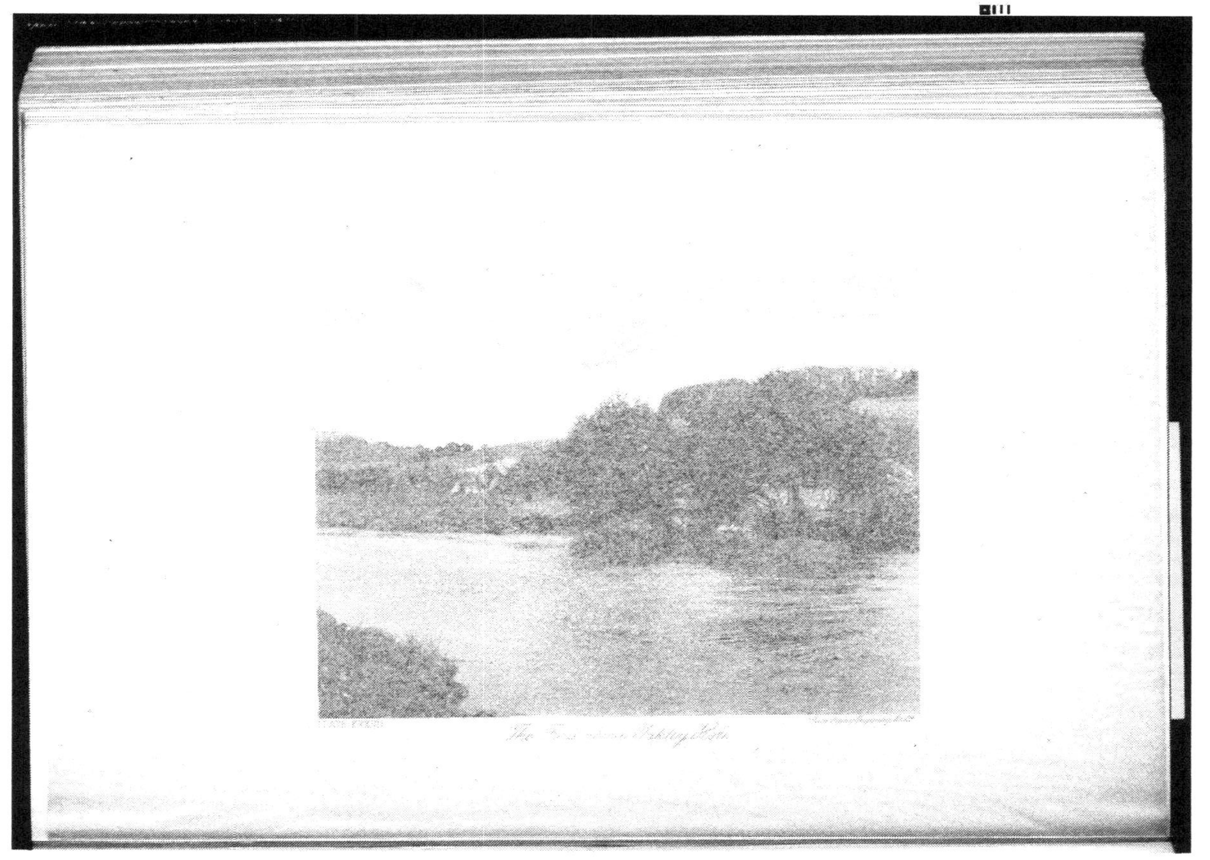

The Tees above Rokeby Park

under the eastern bank has been stopped by a series
of posts and rails.   A short distance below these
posts and rails there is a rough run close to the
opposite bank, and the general appearance of this
part of the Test is fairly portrayed in Plate XXXVII.

Just below this rough run a good fish was feeding
and splashing about, and as the distance was quite
twenty-five yards, I wondered if I could put a fly over
it with the wind blowing downstream and towards
my bank.   After a few attempts the cast came off, and
the fish came at the fly with a rush, and when hooked
started downstream under the opposite bank at a
great pace.

Having to clamber over a rough kind of fence to
follow it on my bank, I slacked at once, handed the
rod to the keeper until I was over the fence, and then
took the rod from his hands.   When a fish feels the
line slack it generally sinks down in the water and
remains fairly quiescent, and this one was no exception to the rule.   The moment I tightened on it,
another rush—this time upstream—made my reel
sing, until I feared that I should have to clamber
back over the fence for fear of having all my line
run out.

At length it turned and again tore downstream,
all the time being almost under the far bank.
Gradually I got on terms with it, and in a few minutes
we could see a large fish fighting deep down in Oakley
Hole.   Naturally it tried its level best to hang me
up in every weed-bed, but the continual strain at last

began to tell, and the exhausted fish was deftly lifted out by the keeper in the landing-net.

A tap on the head with the *priest* resulted in its throwing up six or seven minnows, and a careful scrutiny of the contents of its mouth and the upper part of the gullet failed to give the smallest indication of anything like insect life, so that it must be confessed that clearly, although it took the male welshman's button, it was not at the moment feeding on the natural insects which this pattern is intended to represent. Plate XXXVIII. is a reproduction of the photograph I took of this beautiful brace of fish shortly after the second, which weighed 2 lbs. 14 oz., was killed.

On the 10th June two more trout of 1 lb. 10 oz. and 1 lb. 5 oz. were taken with the button, but a third rising fish would not look at it, and eventually fell victim to a dark olive dun female—a very well-conditioned male trout of 2 lbs. 2 oz. This was the end of the so-called mayfly season, or what in modern times we shall have to rename the welshman's button season, of 1909.

ified

in its
careful
upper
ication
e con-
welsh-
ing on
died to
of the
of fish
14 oz.

10 oz.
but a
ntually
ry will-
was the
modern
button

began to tell, and the exhausted fish was deftly lifted out by the keeper in the landing-net.

A tap on the head with the *priest* resulted in its throwing up six or seven minnows, and a careful scrutiny of the contents of its mouth and the upper part of the gullet failed to give the smallest indication of anything like insect life, so that it must be confessed that clearly, although it took the male welshman's button, it was not at the moment feeding on the natural insects which this pattern is intended to represent. Plate XXXVIII. is a reproduction of the photograph I took of this beautiful brace of fish shortly after the second, which weighed 2 lbs. 14 oz., was killed.

On the 10th June two more, one 1 lb. 10 oz., and 1 lb. 5 oz., were taken with the button, but a third rising fish would not look at it, and eventually left off rising, and was caught on the 11th—a very well-conditioned trout, most artistically spotted. This was the end of the so-called mayfly season, or what in modern times we shall have to rename the welshman's button season, of 1905.

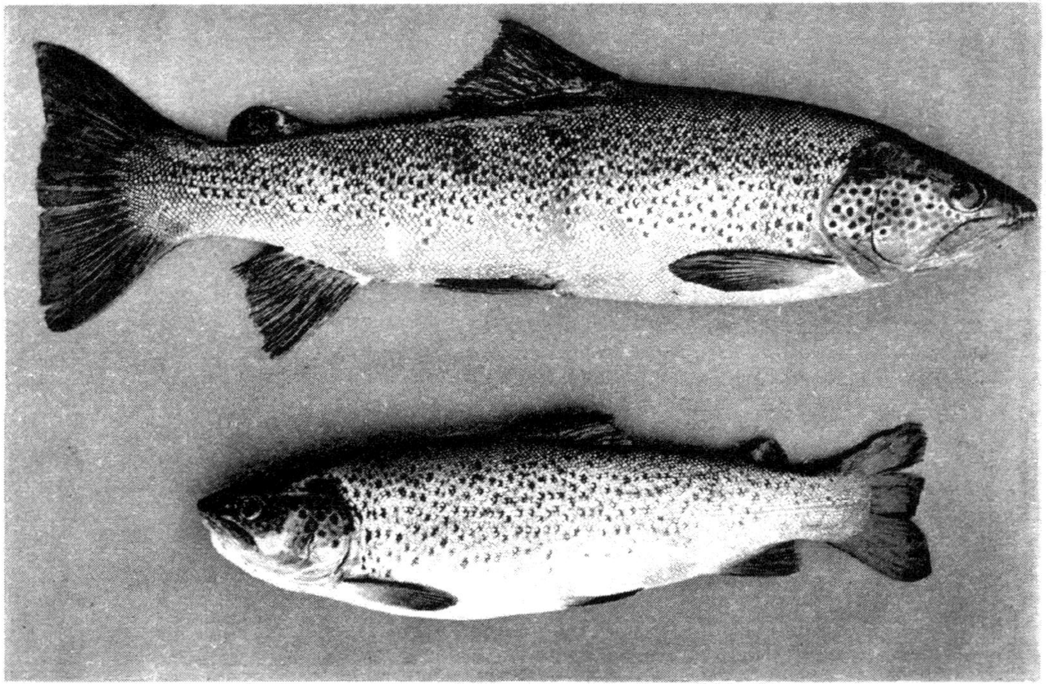

PLATE XXXVII

A Brace of Test Trout

Swan Electric Engraving Co.

CHAPTER VII

EVENING FISHING

THE opinion that Test trout-fishing is all over by the end of June was freely expressed by some witnesses at the inquiry held in Southampton, in May 1906, in reference to the application from the Avon and Stour Fishery Board to include the Test, Itchen, and other Hampshire streams in their district. Such an opinion has, as far as I know, never been seriously enunciated in respect to the Itchen, because from time immemorial the banks of that beautiful stream have been frequented and fished on fine summer evenings by enthusiastic dry-fly men, whose patience has sometimes been rewarded by good sport.

The evening rise is of many sorts and conditions. The first and most usual, if my readers will pardon the solecism, is that during which there is no fly and no rise. Given fly *on* the water the fish will rise, but the angler must not imagine because he sees swarms of spinners in the air, males indulging in that giddy dance which they most affect, or females waiting for a favourable opportunity to complete their life's work and deposit their eggs, that he is in for a good time.

If, as the sun sets, the wind does not rise and the temperature does not fall too much, he may expect

that the females will decide to lay their eggs and fall
on the water with outstretched wings, in an exhausted
or dying state.   Sometimes it would appear as if
every fish in the water, large or small, is feeding madly
in the early part of the evening, coming to the surface
and ploughing up the water in all directions.   Wherever the fisherman stands he can cover many fish, all
seemingly intent on taking a full evening meal before
retiring for the night.

It may be that the trout are taking pale watery
duns or blue-winged olives while he is trying spinners, or they may be taking the sherry spinners,
male or female, while he is trying the spinners of the
olive or iron blue   As a rule, although the fish are
evidently well on the feed, such evenings are most
disappointing, and more often than not the fisherman
gets a blank, or at best returns two or three finger-
lings, instead of scoring among the *sockdollagers*, as
Francis Francis so aptly named them

The most probable reason of his ill-success is that
he is excited and flurried, keeps moving from one
feeding fish to another, seldom placing his fly accurately, and continually moving upstream to cast to a
fresh fish.   He is in such a hurry that he does not
even dry his fly, and after a few minutes has become
so utterly demoralised that he cannot differentiate
the rise of a yearling from that of a three-pounder.
Another reason for the non-success of the dry-fly man
on such an evening often is that the fish are taking
the nymphs under water, and not feeding at all on

floating insects. The advice to give to a beginner
is that he should spot a good fish rising well and stick
to it until he has either pricked it or set it down.

Every parent is proud of his own offspring, and I
hope therefore to be forgiven for the conceit of believing
that the artificial flies dressed according to the modern
notions are far more killing than the standard patterns
used in earlier times. If the fish are taking upright
winged flies, either of the sexes of the pale watery
dun or the blue-winged olive will probably rise the
trout or grayling. If what they are taking is invisible,
it may be inferred that the spent or ovipositing females,
or in exceptional cases the spent males, are on the
water, and the olive, pale watery, iron blue, or sherry
spinners will be the most likely flies.

A fish rising under or close to the bank on which
the fisherman is standing (or, better still, kneeling)
is far more likely to fall a victim than one in mid-
stream. As a rule, it is difficult to float the fly over
a trout rising under the opposite bank without drag,
and the smallest amount of drag is sufficient to set
a big fish down, even when well on the feed. It is
unwise to select a fish rising in such a position that
an abnormally long cast is required, the more so as
one's judgment of distance is apt to be at fault in the
waning light, the general tendency being to place the
fly beyond the centre of the ring made by the rise,
and let the upper part of the collar, or even the reel
line, drag over the fish and thus set it down.

The ideal rising trout to select is one under the

angler's bank, in a place where the river is flowing from west to east, so that the angler is looking up into the best of light. Light is a very important factor, and a man cannot by any possibility see his fly on the surface of the water if he is standing with his back to the sun which has just dipped below the horizon. Besides, the lengthy shadow cast by it of his manly form and proportions is likely to scare every shy trout within many yards.

It is at all times a good policy to be severe on hooked fish, and especially so in the evening or when they are of great average size. A big fish when first hooked seems to reflect for a fraction of a second before starting on its run, and if during this short space of time its head is resolutely turned downstream, and the angler keeps it in this downward course, it is more often than not brought successfully to the net. In fact, when dealing with large trout it may be enunciated as an axiom that either the fish bullies the fisherman or the fisherman bullies the fish, and in this respect, above all, keep your mind well fixed on the principle that *Ce n'est que le premier pas qui coûte.*

The blue-winged olive (*Ephemerella ignita*) is an insect which at any time after the end of June is likely to be hatching out of an evening in the subimago state. In former times its imitations were seldom successful, and this very probably was due to their being so unlike the natural fly, especially in colour. The patterns as now dressed are generally acceptable to both fish and fisherman, and when the shy trout of the Test or Itchen are feeding in the gloaming on this striking-looking insect, these imitations are usually found efficacious in tempting some of them to their destruction.

I remember well that on a July evening when, after a hot day with south-westerly wind, the air was calm and genial, and at about eight o'clock I found myself in a smooth and rather slow-running reach of the Oakley stream, where a fish was rising steadily, and with little disturbance of the surface I tried a variety of spinners without result, and presently, catching sight of a blue-winged olive floating down, and seeing the fish quietly annex it, I changed my fly to one of the males. The fish was feeding close to the opposite bank, and with plenty of slack line I managed to put the fly over it, and it sailed down without the smallest appearance of drag.

The trout rose, fastened, plunged headlong into a weed-bed, was worked out of this by hand, and the moment I got a pull at it with the rod, promptly put its head down and tail up and was buried in another tangle of vegetation. Once more the fish was handed out, and again and again it repeated these tactics, until at length it gave in and was gently towed into the landing-net—a handsome male of 2 lbs. 2 oz.

A friend was fishing with me on that day, and not being at that time a believer in the new patterns, he had rigidly adhered to his old favourites, and fished the entire day and evening with them—only succeed-

ing in landing and returning four undersized fish. I
did not cast a fly before eight o'clock, and killed the
one just referred to and lost another with the same
pattern. I rather fancy that since that day my friend,
who is a first-rate performer, has added the blue-
winged olive to his list of killing patterns.

After another fine warm day in the same season
it turned cold in the evening, but here and there
a fish was rising, and although it was rather early in
the season for that fly, yet a few subimagines of
Ephemerella ignita were present. I put up the male,
and hooked a fish which I could see was a large grayling. It tore about in all directions, and if I had been
alone it is doubtful if I could have landed it. The
keeper, however, managed to put the net under it,
and we found that it was hooked in the dorsal fin,
and weighed 2 lbs. 14 oz. After this I landed a
brace of trout with the same pattern, both males,
2 lbs. 10 oz. and 1 lb. 9 oz., so had altogether a
very pretty evening's sport.

The male and female of the blue-winged olive
share the honours about equally in my diary. On
the 2nd July 1906 I could not get the semblance
of a rise to the male, so after trying the spinners
of the olive and iron-blue and the female sherry
spinner (this latter being the imago of *Ephemerella
ignita*), I changed to a female blue-winged olive, and
secured a handsome female trout of 2 lbs. 9 oz.
On the 3rd July 1907 the diary records a brace of
trout taken with the female, weighing respectively

1 lb. 9 oz. and 1 lb. 15 oz. The male was successful on the 20th July 1908 in killing a trout of 2 lbs. 15 oz., and on the 31st of the same month three sizable grayling and a trout of 1 lb. 7 oz. were taken with the female; while on the 3rd August another good trout of 2 lbs. 8 oz. was again killed with the female.

The year 1909 was a poor one for the spinners, as the evenings were seldom calm and practically never mild, and hence I am inclined to believe that without a good pattern of the blue-winged olive the evening fishing would have turned out quite disastrous. From the middle of August to the middle of September almost all the trout killed in the evenings were taken with one of the sexes of this fly. The peculiarity of the season, however, was that the largest of the trout never seemed to come on to surface food, so that the average size of most Test fishermen's bags was distinctly below that of previous years. I killed, however, with the pattern referred to trout of 2 lbs. 11 oz, 2 lbs., 2 lbs, and many others from this weight down to the limit of $1\frac{1}{4}$ lb

The pale watery spinner, like the dun or sub-imago stage of the same insect, is decidedly a better killer on the Itchen than on the Test, so that to give the reader any experiences of the success of this pattern it is necessary for me to go back a few years. July of 1903 was a bad month on the Itchen; heavy rain and south-westerly gales prevailed, and there was scarcely a single warm, calm, genial evening such as is desirable for fishing the spinners with success. The 14th, however, was one of those evenings when every trout in the river seemed to be feeding freely, and the surface of the stream was covered by the breaks of rising fish. In other words, it was the class of evening, referred to in an earlier part of this chapter, which often makes the disappointed angler feel as if he could destroy his tackle and give up dry-fly fishing altogether, so indignant does he feel at his inability to rise a decent-sized fish. After trying in succession every pattern of olive and iron-blue spinner, black gnat, and brown ant without a response, in despair I tied on a pale watery spinner female, and in the last few minutes during which the light was good enough to enable me to see the fly floating on the surface, I succeeded in capturing three good trout of 1 lb. 2 oz., 1 lb. 3 oz., and 1 lb. 9 oz.

The bad weather continued well into August, and on the 10th I paid a visit with a good friend to Winnall, where, as had happened so many times before, the lessee had been kind enough to offer me a few days From ten in the morning until nearly seven o'clock in the evening we scarcely saw a feeding fish. I then landed and returned a trout of about 1 lb. with the female pale watery spinner. Walking slowly up the river, I arrived at a part of the main stream where the river flows under a railway bridge, and then in a deep long bay under the western bank on which I was standing. A fish rose, with little disturbance of the surface, close to the bank in a run of about eighteen inches in width, with a heavy weed-bed just outside it.

At the first cast the little spinner was taken, and almost instantaneously the fish jumped and landed on the bank, and in another moment jumped back into the river and tore along into the weed-bed. I slacked at once, took the line in my hand and persuaded the trout out of the weeds, and getting a fair pull on it with the rod, landed a perfect female of 2 lbs 1 oz. Twice before in my dry-fly experiences of over thirty years had a hooked trout jumped ashore. The first got off, the second was ignominiously skull-dragged along the meadow, and after the fashion related the third was killed. In the *Field* of April 9, 1898, under the title of "History Repeated," the account of the two previous instances of hooked trout jumping on to the bank was given *in extenso*

The female olive spinner or representation of the ovipositing imago gave me a very good evening once on the Itchen in May. It had been a fine hot day, with scarcely any hatch of fly, and southerly wind. Late in the afternoon it grew dull, and at sunset the sky was of a heavy leaden hue with threatening thunder-clouds all round the horizon. There were a few, but very few, olive spinners just dipping the tail end of their bodies in the water so as to wash off and deposit at each dip a few of their eggs. With very careful fishing I caught three trout of 1 lb. 6 oz., 1 lb. 3 oz., and 1 lb. 2 oz., and then changing to a pale watery spinner female, as the next

fish would not look at the olive, secured a nice fish of
1 lb. 3 oz.

Fine, hot, sunny days were numerous during the
summer of 1906. On one of them from 10 A.M. to
7.30 P.M. there was scarcely a movement to be
seen, and, in fact, it really was not worth while
attempting to fish. Just as the sun began to dip
below the distant horizon, the air was full of female
spinners, chiefly spent red-bodied olives, and sherry
spinners ovipositing, and the fish came steadily on
to the rise as soon as these spinners settled down
on the water. With the olive (red) spinner female
at the second cast a strong, active fish was hooked,
severely handled, and landed in a few minutes—a
very handsome male trout of 2 lbs. 14 oz.

The moment the fly was extracted from this trout's
mouth it was carefully dried and presented to another
fish, which promptly rose, fastened, rushed off at a
great pace, and succeeded in shaking out the little
hook. After a few more casts, a second trout—a
female of 2 lbs. 5 oz.—was secured, and then, although
the fish were still rising well, they could not be tempted
with the fly on the cast. I changed at once to a
sherry spinner female, a fish of about 1¼ lb. was
landed and returned, and then a third—a male of
2 lbs. 5 oz.—was added to the take. The rise was
then all over, and as the result of less than a quarter
of an hour's work a leash of perfect Test trout,
weighing in the aggregate 7 lbs. 8 oz., was sent off
that evening to regale some friends in London.

PLATE XXXIX

Typical Dry Bog Winter

Swan Electric Engraving Co.

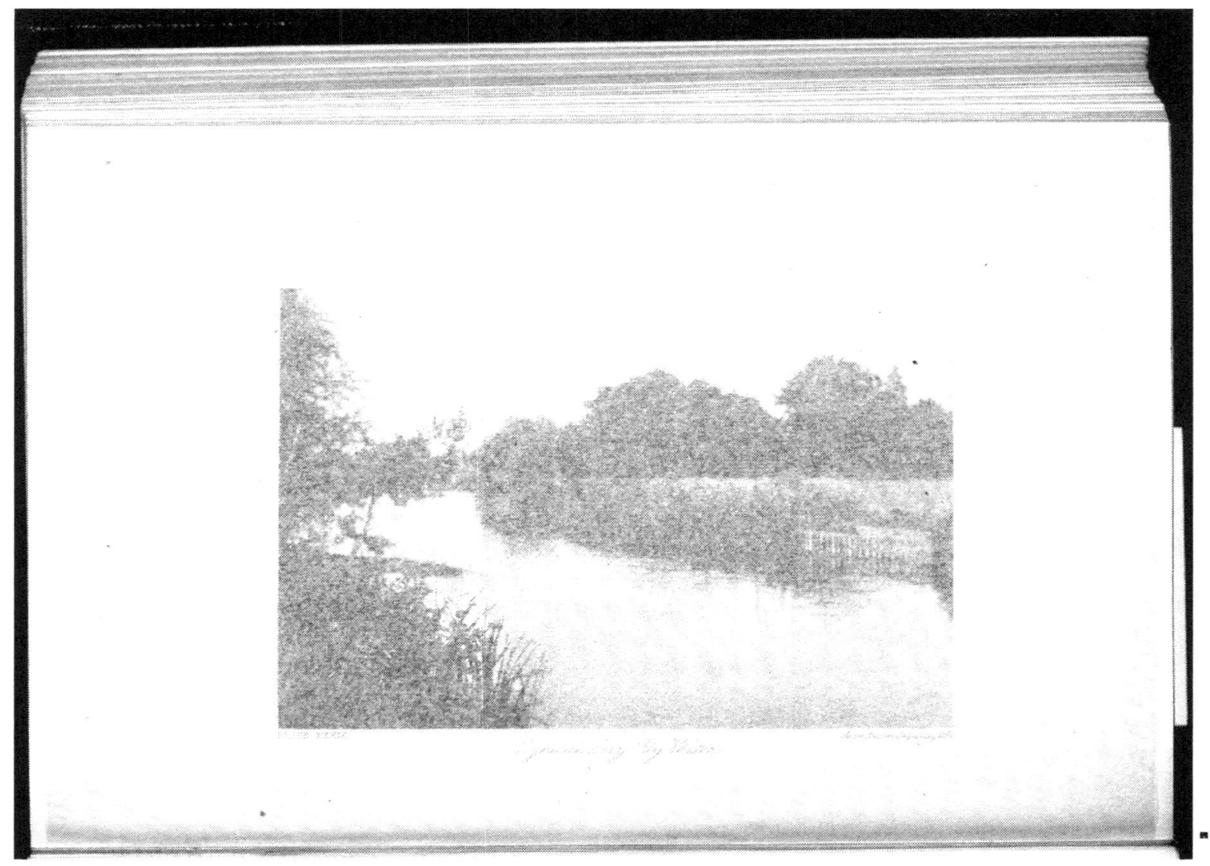

[illegible] by Water

On August 4th, another fine fresh day, when no rising fish could be seen while the sun was shining, the female sherry spinners, each carrying its little round ball of blue-green eggs, were out in clouds during the evening. In due course, after dropping their eggs, they fell on the water, and were greedily taken by the hungry fish. Such a rise never lasts many minutes, and I esteemed myself most fortunate in killing three trout of 3 lbs., 1 lb. 12 oz., and 1 lb. 14 oz., besides returning two more of about 1 lb. each, with the sherry spinner female during these few minutes The place where these and the leash mentioned before were taken is, to my mind, a typical bit of dry-fly water, and Plate XXXIX., I think, does fair justice to it.

There are, of course, evenings when the feeding fish are taking the male spinners when they are plentiful, and when they are floating down on the water in an exhausted condition with wings outstretched, and almost lifeless. The Ephemeridæ, when they first begin hatching out in the subimago stage, are nearly all males, and as a natural consequence the first to shuffle off the subimaginal envelope and emerge as spinners are also nearly all of the male sex. The females of each particular batch deposit their ova and end their short aerial life before the clouds of males, this being nature's provision to ensure the presence of males to fertilise the ova of the latest of the females in the batch. Thus when there are, as usually happens, consecutive batches of females, the males will be plentiful, and many of them end their short existence between the successive batches of the subimagines.

Such a state of things must have existed one July evening, when two of my friends were fishing as my guests, and I was walking with them. The fish rose fairly well, and one of my friends could not find a fly to tempt them, although to my certain knowledge he tried every pattern of female spinner. When the other friend and the keeper rejoined us at the hut after all was over, he reported that he had put up the sherry spinner male and had killed a brace of trout, 1 lb. 12 oz. and 2 lbs., besides losing three other sizable fish and killing a small grayling.

I had a somewhat similar experience on the 2nd September 1909, when, after a fine day with south-easterly wind, the evening was also fine but cold. There were very few flies on the water, and as a natural sequence few fish rising. After trying both sexes of the blue-winged olive, and the sherry spinner female, I eventually put up the male and at once killed a good trout, a male of 1 lb. 10 oz., and two grayling.

With the sherry spinner female I have had some very good evenings, but perhaps one of those which most appealed to me was on the Itchen in July. I had spent the day with two of the best of sports-men on one of the upper reaches, and the day had been showery with light southerly wind. We had all killed a few fish during the daytime, my own

contribution to the day being three trout of 4 lbs.
7 oz. The evening turned out very hot and muggy,
and I was on a small tributary stream which always
holds some big fish, and where they have deservedly
the reputation of being extraordinarily shy and difficult
to tempt.

Close under the bank on which we were standing,
a good fish rose very quietly two or three times, so I
put a pale watery spinner female over it, without result.
Then an iron-blue spinner female, and then again a
sherry spinner male ; still with no response. I then
knotted on a sherry spinner female, and at the very
first cast the fish rose, and the moment it was hooked,
ran straight down under my feet and into a weed-
patch. I succeeded in working it out by hand, and
at once it went off again down some fifteen yards into
another weed-bed. Down I ran below it, after slacking, and once more worked it out by hand, and at
length netted a beautiful female trout of 2 lbs. 14 oz.,
quite a notable fish for the Itchen.

The 28th August 1906 was a day selected by a
good friend for me to pay a visit to his water, and
although, of course, he told me to kill any sizable
trout, the great reason why he asked me to pay attention to a particular part of the water was that he
thought there were too many grayling in it, and he
wanted as many killed as possible. In the morning
I went straight down to the place where the grayling
were generally found, and without much difficulty
spotted the iron-blue dun male as the most plentiful

N

fly on the water. With one of the imitations of this
I worked steadily and patiently for some hours over
a batch of some seven or eight rising fish, and eventually killed five of them, all grayling, two undersized
and the remainder fish of 1 lb. 4 oz., 1 lb. 2 oz., and
1 lb. 8 oz.

After a cup of tea the keeper and I started for a
part of a side stream where my host thought there
were also too many grayling. It was deep and slow-
running water, and had been closely piled and sheathed
with timber down both banks. Nearly all the plank-
ing had been washed away at different times, so that
there were formidable-looking piles standing well up
above the water at a varying distance from the bank
—some within a foot or so, and others a yard or a
yard and a half out from it. I put up a brown ant
and killed a dace, and finding that this fly would
not rise any other feeding fish, changed to a sherry
spinner female, with which I killed a small grayling.

Just opposite one of the piles a good fish was feeding occasionally, and getting myself well down and
fishing with the horizontal cast, I managed to put the
fly over it after a few attempts. One has to keep
well down in such a place so as to be out of sight, and
it is necessary to be very patient under such conditions, and cast only at long intervals. The fish rose
slowly and sucked in the fly, and I struck with the
utmost deliberation. I noted that it was a good trout,
and not a grayling as I expected, and it plunged down
deep into the water, so that I had the greatest diffi-

culty in getting on terms with it. Every time I
forced it up to the surface it at once turned over,
and standing on its head, fought its way down again.
This was repeated over and over again, and as the
fish was gradually drawn downstream, the keeper with
his net in hand patiently followed me, taking in every
detail of the situation. Presently the trout began to
give in, and just as I was bringing it in to the net
it made one final plunge and the hook came away.
Almost at the same moment the keeper, like a flash
of lightning, reached out at arm's length and secured
the fish, a male of 2 lbs. 7 oz.

I really had qualms of conscience as to whether I
ought to kill the fish or return it, the more so that
it was on a friend's water ; but as it was a male, after
a few moments' consideration I decided to kill it.
If it had been a female I should certainly have returned it for the benefit of the fishery. It was a
satisfaction to me later on to find that my host
approved of my action.

CHAPTER VIII

SEDGES

Any one of the old school of dry-fly men, if asked his opinion of sedge fishing, would probably reply that he rated it as perhaps the easiest and least sporting style of chalk-stream fishing, and very likely would add that, as the trout of the Test and Itchen do not feed on these caddis-flies until very late in the evening or after dark, it should not be considered a test of skill on the angler's part to delude them into taking his artificial flies. I confess to having been myself in the past an exponent of this theory, and should have been a firm adherent to it to-day but for the experiences I had in 1907.

During that summer, the evenings when the trout rose at the spinners were few, so much so that at the end of June I had serious thoughts of abandoning the river until the following spring. A certain amount of *amour propre*, however, spurred me on to persevere and devote some time to the study of the habits of the fish during the daytime in the hot weather. I noticed that there was generally a fair sprinkling of sedge flies in the grass on the river-banks, and during the afternoons there were frequently odd ones to be seen dipping on the surface

and depositing their eggs. Most of the evenings
turned cold and frosty, so that there were few if any
caddis-flies to be seen at or after the hour of sunset,
when one would have expected to see the majority
of them. Still, sedge fishing in the daytime gave me
such good sport that I am tempted to describe some
examples of it.

On the afternoon of the 1st July in that year I
saw two dark sedges taken by a fish in broad daylight,
and putting up the small dark sedge pattern, got into
position, and with the utmost care put it over the
rising fish. A bold rise and a rush from a strong fish,
and a pretty 2 lb. trout was in the net.

After waiting a short time I caught sight of
another rise, and although I did not positively see
the fly, yet felt sure that the fish had taken one of
the same little sedges. Another pause to study the
situation, and getting well down in position, again
I despatched the small dark sedge on its errand.
Another rise, and a second trout of 1 lb. 8 oz. was
landed.

A little later, once more a fish rising shyly and at
long intervals was cast over, and it like its two pre-
decessors rose and was killed—weight, 2 lbs. 4 oz.
Total for the afternoon, three trout, 5 lbs. 12 oz.
After this, whenever I saw sedges ovipositing during
the afternoon I waited until a trout taking them could
be seen, spotted the fish most carefully, and very often
succeeded in tempting it. I found that the small
dark sedge and the medium sedge were about equally

efficacious, so I made it a rule to secure one of the natural insects, and if it was a small dark-coloured one I put up the small dark sedge, and if it was a trifle larger and paler in colour I used the medium sedge as the pattern to be tied on the cast.

On the 6th July I had a very good afternoon, and killed in rapid succession, without moving far, two brace of perfect Test trout with the small dark sedge. They were, respectively, a female 2 lbs. 7 oz., a male 2 lbs. 9 oz., a male 2 lbs. 6 oz., and a female 2 lbs. 8 oz., or 9 lbs. 14 oz the aggregate weight of the four.

On the 8th, a dull day with some light rain and occasional heavy squalls, the medium sedge tempted one—a male of 1 lb. 15 oz. After this I could not get a rise, although several fish were taking fly on the surface, so I changed to the small dark sedge, and with it killed two female trout, 2 lbs. 5 oz. and 2 lbs. 10 oz. Then again I could not get a rise, so changed back to the medium sedge, and killed a fourth of 1 lb. 14 oz., a female.

I was then fishing just above the hut, on a stretch of rough water which is shown on Plate XL. A big fish rolling up at something on the surface caught my eye, and after some little consideration I decided on the spot from which the attack should be made. After a few attempts the fly was accurately placed, and the fish fastened at once. It ran upstream at a fair pace, and the moment I got a good strain it began turning over and over in the water and dropping

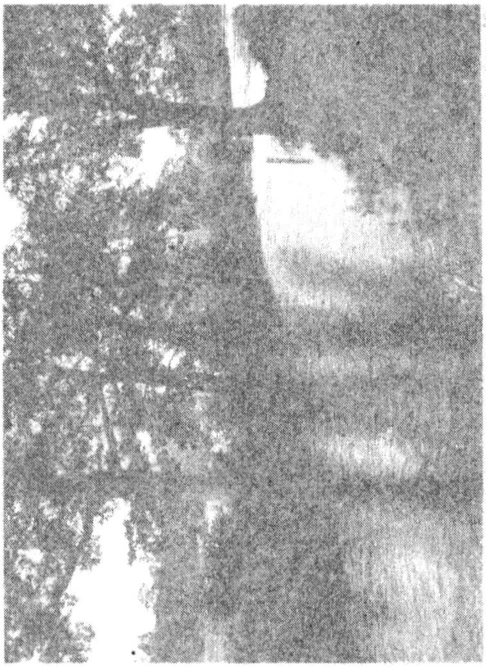

efficacious, so I made it a rule to secure one of the natural insects, and if it was a small dark-coloured one I put up the small dark sedge, and if it was a trifle larger and paler in colour I used the medium sedge as the pattern to be tied on the cast.

On the 6th July I had a very good afternoon, and killed in rapid succession, without moving far, two brace of perfect Test trout with the small dark sedge. They were, respectively, a female 2 lbs. 7 oz., a male 2 lbs. 9 oz., a male 2 lbs. 6 oz., and a female 2 lbs. 8 oz., or 9 lbs. 14 oz. the aggregate weight of the four.

On the 8th, a dull day with some light rain and occasional heavy squalls, the medium sedge tempted one—a male of 2 lbs. 15 oz. After this I could not get a rise, although several fish were taking fly on the surface, so I changed to the small dark sedge, and with it killed two females, one 2 lbs. 9 oz. and 2 lbs. 10 oz. Then again I could not get a rise, so changed back to the medium sedge, and killed a fourth of 1 lb. 14 oz., a female.

I was then fishing just above the hut, on a stretch of rough water which is shown on Plate XL. A big fish rolling up at something on the surface caught my eye, and after some little consideration I decided on the spot from which the attack should be made. After a few attempts the fly was accurately placed, and the fish fastened at once. It ran upstream at a fair pace, and the moment I got a good strain it began turning over and over in the water and dropping

PLATE XI.

Rough Water above the Hut.

down to me. I kept it moving downwards, and after a very short interval it was in the net. I never remember to have seen a heavy fish make so poor a fight, and when we looked at it both the keeper and I were astonished at its condition. It was an abnormally short, deep, thick female trout, and turned the scale at 3 lbs. 10 oz. I only wish that in those days I had better understood the photographing of fish, as it was a specimen worthy of being reproduced. Total for the afternoon, 5 trout, 12 lbs. 6 oz.

The medium sedge scored on the 9th July with three trout, a male 3 lbs. 3 oz., a male 2 lbs. 6 oz., and a female 1 lb. 8 oz., and the small dark sedge accounted for a fourth, another female of 1 lb. 14 oz.—four trout in all, weighing 8 lbs. 15 oz. Thus on these four afternoons there were killed in all 17 trout, weighing 36 lbs. 15 oz. Every one of these fish was in the pink of condition, and with the solitary exception of the big one of 3 lbs. 10 oz., every one fought like a demon Candidly, never before did I have such sport under such conditions; and although I have done well in subsequent years with sedges in the daytime, the total killed has never approached the figures of those red-letter days in July 1907.

Sedge fishing, according to the established maxims of the dry-fly man, takes place during the late evenings of the summer and early autumn. It may be laid down as an axiom that the best *hatches* take place on calm, mild evenings; and here again the reader must understand that the word *hatch* is a misnomer, applied by the angler to the appearance on the water of the various species and genera of Trichoptera or caddis-flies, usually grouped together and called sedge flies. It is perhaps not necessary here to recapitulate the origin of the three patterns in the present series, as this branch of the subject was duly discussed in a previous chapter.

The three flies have been named the small dark sedge, medium sedge, and cinnamon sedge, and are numbers 31, 32, and 33 in the series. When the prevailing fly is a smallish one and dark in hue, such as *Goera pilosa* male, the first is the pattern to select. When medium-coloured and medium-sized flies, such as the female of *Goera pilosa*, or *Rhyacophila dorsalis*, are on the water, the second is to be preferred. In the presence of the sandy-coloured large sedges with mottled or blotched wings, such as *Limnophilus lunatus*, the last and largest sedge fly in the series is most likely to be successful.

The advice given in the chapter on evening fishing, to select a fish rising in a good light, is all-important ; the fly must be quite dry and floating ; and one of the golden rules to observe is to get the length of line required to cover the fish as accurately as possible, and to cast just as delicately, and just as accurately, and just as seldom as one should when fishing in broad daylight.

The first season of my fishing the particular part of the Test specially referred to throughout these chapters was 1905, and on the 1st July in that year, a warm, fine day, with light south-westerly wind, there was little or nothing to do during the forenoon, so after a refreshing cup of tea, accompanied by the keeper I walked across to the main river. Soon after our arrival a fish rose, and was tempted by a brown ant on the cast. It was a well-conditioned trout — a female of 1 lb. 12 oz. ; but we had made it our rule that season to return all females under 2 lbs., so back it went, and it is to be hoped has grown and produced a numerous and healthy progeny.

Wandering up and down with our eyes glued to the stream for hours, we literally did not see a single rise, and in fact we both began to despair of saving the blank that evening. Nothing moved until nearly eight o'clock, and then here and there a fish would break the surface, and perhaps not show again for many minutes. The sun gradually dipped and dis-appeared, and there was a little more excitement, as the fish began to feed at shorter intervals. I tried in vain every pattern I could think of—both sexes of every spinner, the blue-winged olive, the pale watery dun, the black gnats, and even the brown ant.

Then, as it was nearly dark, I put up a small dark sedge ; but the result was the same, and the case ap-peared desperate in the extreme. I had then arrived at a point just below Oakley Hole, and suddenly saw two or three large sedges. One was caught, and as well as possible in the waning light it was iden-tified as *Limnophilus lunatus*. At once the cinnamon sedge, which is the imitation made from this self-same insect, was carefully threaded on, and fastened to the end of the cast by the usual Turle knot.

At the place where I was standing the river turned just at the lower end of the deep hole towards the south-east, and there came a succession of plops from something closely tucked in under my own bank. Without showing myself, and thus inevitably scaring the fish, it was impossible to locate it exactly, so I got the keeper to take his stand well above and direct me as well as he could where to place the fly. After a few mistakes it landed right, and I heard a rise, and on raising my hand to strike, was pleased to feel the resistance of a good fish.

It made the best of its way out into the stream, and I ran well ahead of it and pulled it downstream as fast as I could. A hundred yards of this was as much as the trout could stand, because, as is well known to my readers, a fish dragged headlong down-stream is soon out of breath, as the respiratory organs do not work satisfactorily under these conditions. I swung it round to the bank, and the keeper netted out a male of 2 lbs. 11 oz.

I applied a touch of paraffin to the fly to assist in drying it, and then working the rod backwards and forwards in the air to assist the drying process, I came once more to the place from which the fish had just been killed. Five yards higher up, and still close under the bank, another fish was busily engaged in sucking in the sedge flies as they floated down. Again the fly was placed accurately, the fish took, was hooked, and once more I was running downstream in an almost breathless state, and another male of 2 lbs. 14 oz. was added to the basket to make up a brace.

Back again to the lower end of the deep hole with the fly quite dry, and we could hear a fish rising out on the edge of the stream. After some few minutes both the keeper and I simultaneously caught sight of its mark, and again the fly was despatched on its errand. The trout took, ran up at a good pace, was turned, dragged downstream, and just as we fondly imagined that all was well, back came the hook and the fish got away. It was then almost dark, so I gave up and returned, well satisfied with a brace of trout, weighing 5 lbs. 9 oz., for our sport on an un-favourable evening.

Another gratifying evening followed a day during which it rained almost continuously from the early morning until well after sunset. I had made my way down to the hut and settled down to clear off arrears of correspondence, in the hopes of finding an im-provement in the weather later on. At last, when it was nearly eight o'clock, I sallied forth, well protected against the wet, and made my way to the run below the bridge on the Oakley stream described before. We selected that part of the water for two reasons—firstly, because it was not far off; and secondly, be-cause we had seen an exceptionally large fish lying just below the foot-bridge, and had vowed to do our utmost to kill this fish before the season was over.

It was about the most cheerless and wretched

evening that could be imagined—raining more or less heavily, and with a strong south-westerly wind, almost half a gale. We were on the eastern bank, and it was quite half-past eight before we saw a fish move. I put up a small dark sedge, because the few flies to be seen in the air looked dark in colour, and seeing a slight commotion on a rough run, managed to manipulate the fly into position so that it came down this particular run. A rise and a run from a lively trout, and the first, one of 2 lbs., was in the net.

Then in quick succession I hooked and lost two more sizable trout, and by this time had arrived at the point below the bridge from which I could fish the run in which the big fish had been seen. In the rapidly failing light I just managed to catch sight of a break on the water, and saw, or imagined I saw, the head and shoulders of a monster. I fished it with the utmost care, and after covering the place accurately two or three times at longish intervals, at length I saw a rise at or close to my fly. I struck, and a heavy fish simply *ripped* upstream and under the bridge. I managed to stop it, and the fish was there for some seconds, with its tail up and head down, fighting for all it was worth. The greatest strain the little rod could put on was not strong enough to turn the trout downstream, but at the same time was sufficient to prevent its running higher up and probably entangling my line in the piles supporting the little foot-bridge.

Moving my position, I used every endeavour to

turn the fish sideways, as this is a plan which very
frequently succeeds when a direct pull is not efficacious. A hint under such conditions is always to
apply the strain on the side towards which the fish's
head is inclined. At last the trout began to drop
downstream, tail first, but no pressure that the rod
could exert was enough to turn it and get it on the
run head-first downstream. I then for the first time
realised the position, and was quite sure that the trout
was hooked foul somewhere in what the sailor would
term *the after part of it.*

Presently the fish got below me, and I held it
with all the strength I could muster, while it swung
round to the bank with its head downstream, and we
gradually worked it into the net. It was not the
monster, but a very handsome female trout of 2 lbs.
15 oz., and it was hooked in the anal fin. As said
before, history has a way of repeating itself, and this
was the third occasion in my long experience of the
dry fly that I had hooked and killed a big trout
hooked in the anal fin.

How does a fish get hooked there if it is rising
at the fly? My theory is that the fish takes the fly
slowly, and the fisherman, as too often happens, is
excited and strikes too quickly. The fly is pulled
down from the fish's mouth, and in the majority of
instances the fish is not hooked at all, or a scale
or two may be torn away and found on the point
of the hook. Exceptionally one has a stroke of
luck, and the barb is firmly embedded in some

part of the trout's body, or one of the fins, and the fish is killed.

Other fortunate evenings have rewarded the use of the small dark sedge. On one I got three good trout, a female 3 lbs. 1 oz., and two males of 1 lb. 8 oz. and 2 lbs.; and on another in the same year, three more, two females of 1 lb. 8 oz. and 2 lbs. 4 oz., and a male exactly 3 lbs. The handsome male trout of 2 lbs. 4 oz., which is the larger of the two fish portrayed in Plate XLI., owed its undoing to the same fly.

The medium sedge is quite as useful a pattern as the small dark sedge—in fact, as before remarked, it depends on the appearance of the first few natural Trichoptera I see—which pattern is adopted, at any rate for the first attempt. I had three good evenings with it in August 1907—on the 7th four trout, three females each of 1 lb. 10 oz., and a male of 2 lbs. 4 oz ; on the 14th three trout, a female of 1 lb. 8 oz. and two males of 1 lb. 11 oz. and 3 lbs. 7 oz. ; and on the 31st a brace, both females, of 1 lb. 8 oz. and 2 lbs. 8 oz. The nine fish killed on these three evenings thus aggregated in weight 17 lbs. 2 oz., or an average of over 1 lb. 14 oz. per trout killed.

The 14th July 1909 was a fine warm day, with slight south-westerly wind — a day during which there were practically no flies on the water and no fish rising. One naturally expects that after such a day the evening rise is likely to be a good one, on the theory that these well-fed trout of the chalk

PLATE XXI

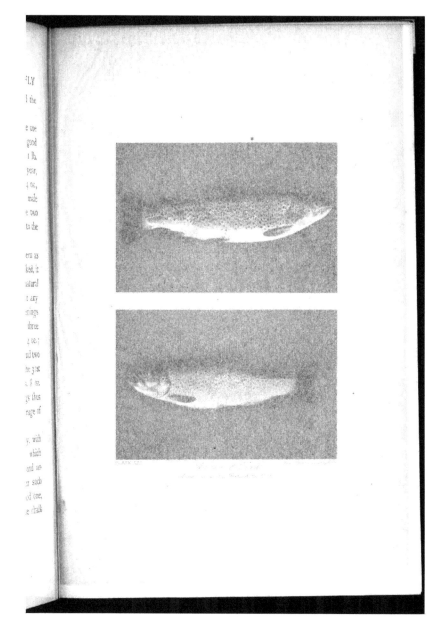

PLATE XLI A Brace of Trout *[illegible]*

Male 20 ℔ 4 oz. Female 11½ ℔ 15 oz.

streams do generally come on the rise for some little time during each day. In this case the evening was dull, with no appearance of blue-winged olive, or spinner of it or of any of the other smaller Ephemeridæ, on the water. Just before dark a few fish began taking an occasional sedge fly, but none of the large trout were on the feed. In rapid succession I killed four with the medium sedge, two females of 1 lb. 15 oz. and 1 lb. 4 oz., and two males of 1 lb. 4 oz. each—the size limit of the water being $1\frac{1}{4}$ lb, so that three of the four were only just sizable. The smaller and better conditioned fish in Plate XLI. is the biggest of this bag.

One of the great charms of the late evening fishing is that one always expects to get the big fish of one's lifetime. Of course, it does not often fall to the lot of mortal to emulate the feat of Major Bartholomew, who during the summer of 1909 killed on the lower Test, with a sedge fly—the old silver sedge, I think— a splendid trout of $8\frac{1}{2}$ lbs., which is believed to be the record fish of the river killed fair and square with dry-fly tackle during the last quarter of a century.

I should like to finish this chapter and this book by conveying a few hints to those of my readers who are not above trying to learn something of the trout and their habits. When prospecting in daytime the angler will occasionally see in a particular place a few extra large fish lying deep down in the water. The very next evening, and possibly for other evenings after that, he is fixed at this spot, and every fish breaking the surface of the water is magnified in his eyes to the proportions of a monster.

It is the opinion of many who have given the subject their careful consideration that these large fish have two apartments—if I may call them so—one the bedroom and the other the dining-room. In its bedroom the trout lies when at home and resting but not feeding, and for its meals adjourns to the *salle à manger*, so that it is almost necessary for the prospector to devote some time to the further study of where these big fish take up their positions when there is a good hatch of fly just coming on. I am quite convinced that somehow the trout and grayling do possess a faculty enabling them to foresee when the plentiful supply of insects for their meal will be present, and they then select the most favourable situation in the vicinity which will enable them to take full advantage of the good things the gods send them.

As an illustration, Plate XLII. is a part of the Oakley stream taken from the western bank, and showing a small bridge crossing the river—above this bridge the water rushes furiously down over a rough incline, and just below the bridge falls over boulders into a deep pool. During the heat of the day one can often see a few large trout in this pool, but during the evening rise the fish feeding there, although sometimes good and sizable ones, are not generally of extra large proportions. When fish are rising, it may be laid down as an axiom that the big ones invariably

breaking the surface of the water is magnified in his eyes to the proportions of a monster.

It is the opinion of many who have given the subject their careful consideration that these large fish have two apartments—if I may call them so—one the bedroom and the other the dining-room. In its bedroom the trout lies when at home and resting but not feeding, and for its meals adjourns to the *salle à manger*, so that it is almost necessary for the prospecter to devote some time to the further study of where these big fish take up their positions when there is a good hatch of fly just coming on. I am quite convinced that somehow the trout and grayling do possess a faculty enabling them to foresee when the plentiful supply of insects for their meal will be present, and they then select the most favourable situation in the vicinity which will enable them to take full advantage of the good things the gods send them.

As an illustration, Plate XLII. is a part of the Oakley stream taken from the western bank, and showing a small bridge crossing the river—above this bridge the water rushes furiously down over a rough incline, and just below the bridge falls over boulders into a deep pool. During the heat of the day one can often see a few large trout in this pool, but during the evening rise the fish feeding there, although sometimes good and sizable ones, are not generally of large proportions. When fish are rising, it may be taken as an axiom that the big ones invariably

PLATE XLII.

View of the Bridge, York.

select the most desirable places and drive away their smaller and weaker brethren. It may be inferred from what has just been said that these extra large fish do not rise in this pool.

About fifty yards below this pool, there is a set of hatches which in olden times regulated the supply of water to irrigation channels. Since those days the value of water meadows has been so decreased in the eyes of both landlords and tenants that most of the irrigation cuts have been allowed to grow up, and the hatches governing the supply of water flowing into them are either out of repair or have been entirely blocked up and are disused. In front of these hatches are the posts, with their heads just projecting above the surface of the river, and under water there are other pieces of rotten or rotting timber which are the débris of the old weed rack.

On these posts the cut weeds accumulate, forming an effective hide for the fish. Immediately below this mass of weeds is a spot where on favourable evenings the big trout generally rise at the spinners and sedges. A few yards lower down is a well-grown withy, and a good screen of bushes, running almost at right angles to the course of the stream. Just below the withy a tunnel or so-called *bunny* under the river carries the water from a ditch draining the low-lying meadows on the western side of the stream.

A narrow concrete sloping parapet, of which there is one on each side of the river across the bunny, forms a precarious path by which a fisherman can, if necessary, follow a hooked fish running downstream. At or after dusk it certainly does not appear a desirable road for the angler, especially as the lower part of the one on the eastern bank is more or less covered by a growth of wild vegetation.

Careful and prolonged scrutiny in the daytime has consistently failed to reveal the presence of the big trout under the weed mass opposite the hatches, or among the remains of the weed rack. I therefore proceeded to search for them elsewhere, and believe that my diagnosis of the case as given before was an accurate one. When there is a good fall of ovipositing or spent spinners or of sedges in the dusk, one or more of these big fish no doubt drops down, takes up its position at the place indicated, and there indulges in its evening meal to repletion.

At the spot where the fish rise the water is smooth and comparatively slow, while in the middle of the river it is much faster, and between the concrete parapets, where the stream is narrowed, the flow is quite rapid, and some forty yards below this there is a small fall over rough boulders where the current is turbulent and the water broken. Plate XLIII. is a reproduction of a photograph of this part of the river from the western bank.

The difficulties of fishing such a spot are certainly formidable. One must cast a very short line of only four or five yards, because it is not possible to take up a position further from the fish. It is never easy to throw a very short line with accuracy and

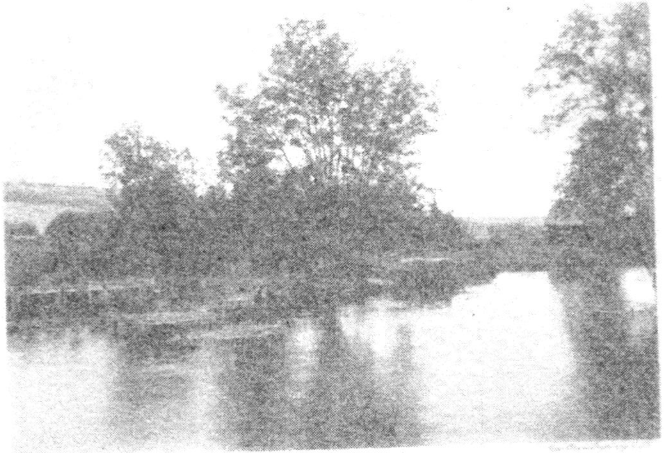

The Feeding Place of the Big Fish

necessary, follow a hooked fish running downstream. At or after dusk it certainly does not appear a desirable road for the angler, especially as the lower part of the one on the eastern bank is more or less covered by a growth of wild vegetation.

Careful and prolonged scrutiny in the daytime has consistently failed to reveal the presence of the big trout under the weed mass opposite the hatches, or among the remains of the weed rack. I therefore proceeded to search for them elsewhere, and believe that my diagnosis of the case as given before was an accurate one. When there is a good fall of ovipositing or spent spinners or of sedges in the dusk, one or more of these big fish no doubt drops down, takes up its position at the place indicated, and there indulges in its evening meal to repletion.

At the spot where the fish rise the water is smooth and comparatively slow, while in the middle of the river it is much faster, and between the concrete parapets, where the stream is narrowed, the flow is quite rapid, and some forty yards below this there is a small fall over rough boulders where the current is turbulent and the water broken. Plate XLIII. is a reproduction of a photograph of this part of the river from the western bank.

The difficulties of fishing such a spot are certainly formidable. One must cast a very short line of only four or five yards, because it is not possible to take up a position further from the fish. It is never easy to throw a very short line with accuracy and

PLATE XLIII

The Feeding Place of the Big Fish

From Chwm Gymru 6.27

delicacy. Drying the fly with a short line after a few attempts soon becomes hard work, and the fish will not take a sunk or sodden fly. One must cast underhanded to avoid the lower branches of the withy. One must strike slowly, because big fish rise slowly. One must strike with sufficient force to drive the hook home in the bony jaws of the trout, and yet not so forcibly as to break the gut. One must be on the alert to keep the hooked fish away from the broken posts and weed rack, out of the weed mass immediately over them, out of the other weed beds in the vicinity, and one has to kill the fish in a comparatively circumscribed area.

I will give briefly three examples of good fish killed there, arranged in chronological order :—The first was on July 28, 1906, a day on which I had set myself to give a fair trial to a new rod which Messrs. Hardy had just made for me, and which had reached me a few days before. It was an inexpensive two-pieced glued cane rod of $9\frac{1}{2}$ feet in length, which I wanted to keep throughout the season in the hut as a spare one to be used in case of accident either to one of my own or my guests' rods.

The day had been fine and hot, the show of spinner during the early evening had been very sparse, and I had not succeeded in killing a single fish. I was slowly wending my way homewards just before dusk, and as usual when passing this place, waited for a few minutes to see if one of the big ones was on the feed. Sure enough there was a rise, and at longish intervals it would be repeated, and the quiet movement could be seen of a good trout just breaking the surface as it quietly sucked down the sedge flies floating down over it.

The medium sedge (dressed, as it always should be, on a No. 2 hook) was quickly knotted on, and as the fish seemed well on the feed the cast was made without delay. The fly, quite dry and cocked, landed about a foot above the fish, which rose slowly, took deliberately, and after an appreciable interval was struck and hooked. Here was a big fish hooked in a place where it had a choice of entanglements, any one of which would suffice to defeat the fisherman and leave the fish victor in the contest.

There was a broken weed rack, with the remains of the posts projecting in the air, just above the fish, masses of weed hanging on the posts, a heavy weed bed in the middle of the river a little higher up. Fifty yards above was a deep pool with rough boulders and endless unconsidered trifles to hang up the line, and on the other bank of the stream, just opposite, there was a series of posts with floating weeds in great numbers fixed on them.

As it has been said, " It is always the unexpected that happens," and instead of trying to foul any of these numerous entanglements, the fish swam out into the centre of the stream and tore down at full speed, until at length I began to think that it would go down over the fall forty yards below, and the only chance of saving the position would be for me to take the risk of following it down on the narrow concrete parapet.

Suddenly it turned and slowly began working up-stream towards me for some distance, then tore down again, and kept on pursuing these tactics, until at length it was brought within the range of the keeper's vision and secured in the landing-net, a very handsome female fish of 3 lbs. 14 oz. I do not think that I ever remember to have put a greater strain on any fish than I did on this one, and the little rod behaved splendidly. After the fight was over it was as straight as it was on the day it left Messrs. Hardy's hands. I should never ask for a better weapon to use to cast any dry fly, even including a mayfly or spent gnat, to any trout in the Test, or to kill it when hooked.

My good friend Senior and another friend (Martin Mosely) were my guests on the second occasion. I was not fishing, but walking first with one and then with the other, and generally enjoying the conversation of both. Their names are both well known in the angling world—Senior as for many years the Angling Editor of the *Field*, and then until the end of 1909 the Editor of that invaluable sporting paper, and a most charming writer under the pseudonym of "Red Spinner"; Martin Mosely has devoted himself in all the time he can spare from his business avocations to the work which has filled the greater part of my life—the study of the insects constituting the surface food of the chalk-stream and other trout.

In such company one could not be dull, and I can

assure the reader that every student of dry fly can learn much by watching such past masters in the art. On this day Mosely had killed a fish of 2 lbs. in the morning, and I elected to accompany Senior during the evening. He did not get a fish during the sparse spinner rise, and at my suggestion put up a medium sedge for the last chance. After killing a pretty fish of 2 lbs. 3 oz. he had almost abandoned any hope of making it a brace, the more so as Mosely presently joined us with a brace of 1 lb. 6 oz. and 1 lb. 8 oz. and announced that the rise was all over for that day.

In despair we went to the old spot opposite to the hatches, and saw a fish there. Of course Senior wanted Mosely to try it, but after some persuasion we induced our old friend to put himself in position and cast to the fish. I had dinned into his ears the necessity of holding on to the fish for all he was worth if he hooked it, as the river was full of weeds and the water level rather low. He promptly hooked the fish, and literally carried out our hint; and it was well he did, as he managed to hold it out of all the dangers, and the keeper eventually landed a beautiful female trout of 3 lbs. 3 oz.

The last and final example I propose giving occurred in August last year. The trout season had been altogether unfavourable, and the cold summer and generally inclement weather had not given many chances of securing big fish during the evenings. The day in question had been showery, and the evening was calm and fine, but there was very little show of spinner, and scarcely any rising fish were to be seen. At the very last moment one was found at the old favourite spot. Once more the medium sedge was the successful pattern, and after a determined and prolonged fight another big trout—a female exactly 3 lbs.—was landed, and enabled the angler to save his blank.

Every true sportsman who fishes the south-country and other chalk-streams should, I think—whether it be a regulation of the fishery or not—make it his invariable rule to give up fishing for the evening as soon as he finds himself unable to distinguish his fly floating down the stream. Nothing that I know of is more certain to make the trout in a fishery preternaturally shy and disinclined to take the artificial than perseverance in casting over feeding fish in the dark.

Fishermen as a class are accused of being far too selfish in the pursuit of their sport, and perhaps we deserve this reproach in many cases. It is not much of a point in our favour to urge that to the majority of our fellow-men—whether fishermen or not—the same charge might often be applied with equal justice Let us, however, one and all show some consideration for the future sport of our brother anglers when fishing the same water as ourselves, and agree to abstain for the future from this most undesirable practice.

At my age it is scarcely probable that I shall write another book. I can honestly say that any experience gained throughout a long apprenticeship has been freely given to the comparatively small section of the public which reads my books, and nothing that I have thought could be of advantage to the angling fraternity has ever been kept back. Many of my readers are my friends; some few have dealt with my theories in a critical, but I hope not hostile spirit; many strangers have corresponded with me at various times on matters connected with our favourite sport. So far as I know, there is not one of them who would call himself my enemy. To one and all let me make my farewell bow, and thank them for their praise, their criticism, their friendship, and their correspondence. Thay have all contributed their share to the interest and pleasure of a comparatively long and happy life.

INDEX

P *

THE END

Printed by BALLANTYNE, HANSON & Co
Edinburgh & London

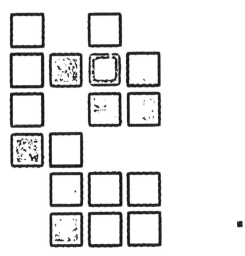

Lightning Source UK Ltd.
Milton Keynes UK
UKHW021913260819
348660UK00005B/495/P

9 781371 329841